Engineers' dispute resolution handbook

By

A SPECIALIST TEAM OF AUTHORS IN KEATING CHAMBERS

Editor: Dr Robert Gaitskell, QC, Eng

Foreword by Professor John Uff, CBE, QC, FREng

thomas telford

ESSEX 15 STREET KEATING CHAMBERS

Published by Thomas Telford Publishing, Thomas Telford Ltd, 1 Heron Quay, London E14 4JD. www.thomastelford.com

Distributors for Thomas Telford books are
USA: ASCE Press, 1801 Alexander Bell Drive, Reston, VA 20191-4400, USA
Japan: Maruzen Co. Ltd, Book Department, 3–10 Nihonbashi 2-chome, Chuo-ku, Tokyo 103
Australia: DA Books and Journals, 648 Whitehorse Road, Mitcham 3132, Victoria

First published 2006

Also available from Thomas Telford Books
Quantifying and managing disruption claims. H. Lal. ISBN 07277 3165 3
Practical adjudication for construction professionals. L Edwards and R. Anderson. ISBN 07277 3109 2
Payment under construction contracts legislation. R. Pettigrew. ISBN 07277 3000 2

A catalogue record for this book is available from the British Library

ISBN: 0 7277 3450 4

© Thomas Telford Limited 2006

Typeset by Academic + Technical, Bristol
Printed and bound in Great Britain by MPG Books, Bodmin, Cornwall

Foreword

Professor John Uff, CBE, QC, FREng

There was a time when the Engineer was King. In those days disputes were, in the first place, settled by the Engineer acting as quasi-arbitrator, usually following his own decision as certifier. Sometimes he changed his mind, and only rarely did a dispute get beyond the contractual mechanism and out into the world of arbitration. And even then the invariably sole arbitrator would be another Engineer, who could be expected to look at the issues in the same way as the original Engineer. Partly for these reasons it was rare for a formal dispute even to arise. Most matters would be dealt with by informal discussion, with the Engineer certifying what he thought was appropriate. Engineers in those days were said to command great respect.

But all was not necessarily well in the world of engineering contracts, even in the heady days of nineteenth century industrialisation. Isambard Kingdom Brunel is still revered as one of the greatest engineering geniuses. But his treatment of contractors shows him in another light. Brunel's appalling treatment of William Ranger, one of the contractors for the Great Western Railway, is fully documented in the report in House of Lords Cases (1854) volume V, page 72. Ranger had taken on a series of contracts including that for the Avon Bridge, which was to be constructed in stone from the tunnels and cuttings eastward of the bridge. Ranger complained that he was deceived by reports as to the nature of the rock, which proved to be much harder than stated. When the project inevitably slowed down, Brunel took the work out of Ranger's hands and charged him with the additional cost of completion as well as delay penalties, eventually driving him to ruin. Ranger's final plea to the House of Lords that Brunel was a substantial shareholder in the company, and for that reason his decision could not be binding, was dismissed with a mixture of disbelief and regret that such a point should be taken. From that stage for more than a century the Engineer remained King.

Ironically, it was not the great power wielded by the Engineer which eventually led to his demise, but something quite different. By the 1970s there was general dissatisfaction in the construction industry that both Engineers and Architects as the principal certifiers of cash flow to Contractors were no longer the independent spirits they once had been. They tended always to err in the Employer's favour, rejecting claims which had then to be pursued in arbitration. Sometimes the Engineer reacted cautiously through fear of being sued himself for overcertification; and sometimes he was under pressure to avoid exceeding budgetary limits of which the Contractor was unaware. Yet under the Institution of Civil Engineers (ICE) standard form conditions of contract, and many others, arbitration against the Engineer's decision could not generally be pursued until after completion of the works, leaving the Engineer in sole charge of the Contractor's cash flow.

In the case of the ICE Conditions of Contract, the first sign of change began with the seemingly innocuous introduction of 'conciliation' as an alternative to the Engineer's decision. One thing rapidly lead to another, the next step being a reduction in the three months allowed for the Engineer's decision, to a more familiar one month. This was followed by the groundbreaking introduction of arbitration available at any time, without the necessity of waiting for completion. This was the situation at the time the Housing Grants, Construction and Regeneration Act came onto the scene in 1996.

No one quite predicted what would be the effect of the statutory adjudication on the construction industry. The ICE initially attempted to preserve the traditional but reduced role of the Engineer by re-labelling the initial 'dispute' as a 'matter of dissatisfaction' so that the Contractor remained bound to submit the matter to the Engineer before a dispute could arise for the purposes of adjudication. This device was considered by some to be legally ineffective, and by others to be contrary to the spirit of the new Act. At all events, it was soon abandoned, leaving hardly a trace of the former regime. The latest 2005 amendments to the main ICE Conditions of Contract, mirrored in all the other ICE forms, thus presents the parties (it must never be forgotten that the Employer may initiate disputes) with a seemingly bewildering choice between negotiation, mediation, adjudication, arbitration or even litigation. All these options must now be packed into any form of construction contract and they present their own challenge to the parties. Rather than searching for a remedy within the inadequate procedures provided up to the 1970s, parties wishing to pursue a genuine dispute now have an *embarras de richesses* in terms of available channels of resolution. The danger thereby created is that the would-be claimant may fail to identify the quickest and cheapest means by which the dispute may be resolved. The prospect of multiple concurrent resolution procedures carries with it the alarming possibility, if not probability, of multiple costs, all of which have to be paid by someone. None of the dispute reformers have yet devised a way of reducing the cost of legal services or the disruption which a formal dispute procedure can cause to normal economic activity.

So there is the challenge that dispute resolution now presents to engineers, contractors, lawyers and all those involved in engineering and construction disputes: how most effectively to make use of the huge variety of available techniques and procedures, and particularly whether to use the procedures singly or in combination. That is why this handbook is now invaluable as a source of essential expertise in making these unavoidable choices. Whatever choice is made, the initiating party inevitably commits to a particular course; and even if that course can be switched before reaching its conclusion, costs will have been incurred which must be paid. Parties must now decide, at the outset of a dispute, their particular strategic route to achieving satisfactory resolution. This presents choices and challenges not dissimilar to those of programming and managing the construction work itself, and involves no less serious outlay of expenditure.

For the task of overcoming these novel hurdles, I am delighted to commend this handbook to anyone embarking on dispute resolution, whether as a theoretical study, in preparation for disputes to come, or in support of actual disputes which need immediate decisions and commitment to a particular course of action. The work is written by a team of specialists who can offer practical help and guidance in all the intricate stages described, and particularly in making the strategic decisions which will ultimately determine whether the dispute is resolved satisfactorily or not. Dispute resolution is no longer to be embarked upon without the guidance offered in this handbook.

John Uff

Keating Chambers
1 January 2006

Contents

Foreword   iii
Professor John Uff, CBE, QC, FREng

Contributors   xiii

1. Introduction   1
Dr Robert Gaitskell, QC

The purpose of this book   1
Overview of the forms of dispute resolution   2
The seven forms of dispute resolution   3
    Final determination procedures   3
    Preliminary determination procedures   4

2. Avoiding disputes   7
Gaynor Chambers

Introduction   7
Contractual means of avoiding disputes   7
    The importance of finalising the contract   7
    Clearly define the scope of the works and quality expected   9
    Ensuring the contract terms are clear and fair   10
    Ensure the dispute resolution clause is well-structured   12
Effective contract management   14

3. When disputes arise   16
Paul Buckingham, Samuel Townend and Jonathan Selby

Overview   16
Initiating a claim   17
    Choosing the dispute procedure   17
    Making the claim   19
Defending a claim   19
    Deadlines   19
Instructing lawyers   21
    Choosing a lawyer   22
    Fees   22
    Agree lines of communication   23
Direct access schemes   24

What is direct access?   24
What are the advantages for clients of using the direct
    access scheme?   24
What types of cases are suited to the scheme?   24
Types of direct access   26
Typical arrangements with a barrister under either of the
    direct access schemes   27

4. **Litigation**   **29**
   Finola O'Farrell, QC

Introduction   29
The Technology and Construction Court system   29
Pre-action protocols   30
Commencement of proceedings   33
   Claim form   33
   Statements of case   33
   Further pleadings   37
   Part 8 claims   38
   Arbitration claims   38
   Adjudication enforcement proceedings   42
Case management   42
Alternative dispute resolution   44
Summary judgment   45
Interim payment   47
Interim injunction   47
Disclosure   48
Witness statements   49
Expert reports   50
Pre-trial review   51
Trial   52
Costs   52
Appeals   55

5. **Arbitration**   **56**
   Paul Buckingham

What is arbitration?   56
Advantages of arbitration   57
Disadvantages of arbitration   58
The arbitration clause   59
   Institutional arbitration   59
   Ad hoc arbitration   59
   Arbitration clause   60
Commencing an arbitration   60
Multi-party claims   61
Choosing an arbitration tribunal   61
Conducting an arbitration   64

Written submissions	64
Documents	64
Factual witnesses	65
Expert witnesses	65
Typical arbitration timetable	66
Ancillary relief	66
The arbitration hearing	66
Preparation	67
Opening submissions	68
Hearing timetable	68
Closing submissions	68
The arbitration award	68
Final award	68
Interest	69
Costs	69
Challenging arbitration awards	70
The 'slip' rule	70
Appeals	71
Procedural irregularity	71
Summary	72

6. Adjudication

Samuel Townend

6. Adjudication	**73**
Introduction	73
The Construction Act and the Scheme	73
Application of statutory adjudication	74
The technical use of adjudication	77
Instalments	77
Notices	77
Ambush adjudications or suspension of work	78
Engineers' fees	79
Rules of adjudication	79
The adjudication notice	80
Appointment of an adjudicator	82
Appointment prior to the dispute	82
Appointment once dispute has arisen	83
The referral notice	83
Costs/offers	85
Request for a meeting or a hearing	86
Responding to adjudication proceedings	86
Obtaining an extension of time	87
Substantive contents of a response	88
Subsequent procedures	89
Written questions	89
Meetings	89
Further submissions	90
The decision	90
Enforcement	90

7. Mediation   92
Robert Evans

What is mediation?   92
Why mediation works   93
Facilitative and evaluative approaches   94
When to use mediation   95
Appointing a mediator: CEDR and other bodies   96
The mediation   97
   The exploration phase   100
   The bargaining phase   101
   The concluding phase   102

8. Expert determination   108
Jonathan Lee

Introduction   108
Expert determination versus other dispute resolution
    processes   110
   Procedure   111
   International agreements   112
Identifying the question that is to be answered   113
The parties' agreement to refer a question to an expert   113

9. Early neutral evaluation   115
Richard Coplin

What it is and when to use it   115
   What is ENE?   115
   Key features of ENE   116
   What does ENE hope to achieve?   116
   What does an evaluator do?   116
   When to use ENE?   117
Appointing an evaluator   117
   Choosing an evaluator   117
   The ENE agreement   117
Preparation for the evaluation   118
The evaluation decision/recommendation   119
Conclusion   119

10. International dispute resolution   120
Dr Robert Gaitskell, QC

Introduction   120
Choosing the dispute resolution procedure   120
Arbitration   121
   Initiating an arbitration   122
   Conducting the arbitration   123
   Challenging and enforcing the award   126
   Arbitration in China   127

Arbitration in Singapore   129
  Arbitration in Malaysia   130
  Arbitration in South Korea   130
  Arbitration in Australia   130
  Arbitration in Taiwan   131
  Arbitration in New Zealand   131
Adjudication and dispute boards   131
  The spread of adjudication   131
  Adjudication in Australia   132
  Adjudication in New Zealand   132
  Adjudication in Singapore   133
  Adjudication in Hong Kong   134
  Adjudication in Malaysia   134
  Dispute boards (serial adjudication)   134
Mediation and early neutral evaluation   135
  The differences between mediation and early neutral
    evaluation   135
  Initiating a mediation   136
Expert determination   137
Conclusion   137
  Controlling the dispute procedure   137
  Making the best use of the outcome   137

11. Immediate help   **143**
Jonathan Selby

The court system and useful resources   143
The court system   143
Precedent   144
Law reporting   145
References   145
Reference sources   146
  Appointing a lawyer   146
Legal resources   146
  Major construction law textbooks   146
  Libraries   147
  Non-subscription websites   147
  Subscription websites   147

12. Conclusion   **149**
Dr Robert Gaitskell, QC

Index   **151**

Contributors

ROBERT GAITSKELL, QC
Silk 1994. Call 1978. Born 1948.
PhD (King's Coll. London).
BSc (Engineering). AKC Chartered
Engineer. Fellow IEE. Fellow IMechE.
FCIArb. Recorder. Former Vice President of the Institution of Electrical
Engineers.
Former Senator of the Engineering Council. CEDR Accredited Mediator.
Adjudication and Arbitration Panel of the IEE.

FINOLA O'FARRELL, QC
Silk 2002. Call 1983. Born 1960.
BA (Dunelm).

ROBERT EVANS
Call 1989. Born 1959.
MA (Cantab). LLB (Lond).
Chartered Engineer.
Member ICE. FCIArb. MHKIE.

JONATHAN LEE
Call 1993. Born 1966.
BEng. AMIEE.

PAUL BUCKINGHAM
Call 1995. Born 1965.
BSc. Chartered Engineer.
Member IChemE.

RICHARD COPLIN
Call 1997. Born 1966.
BA (Oxon).

GAYNOR CHAMBERS
Call 1998. Born 1964.
BSc

SAMUEL TOWNEND
Call 1999. Born 1975.
MA (Cantab).

JONATHAN SELBY
Call 1999. Born 1977.
BA (Cantab).

1. Introduction

Dr Robert Gaitskell, QC

The purpose of this book

Engineers have to wear many hats. They have great technical expertise and can move mountains, bridge rivers, construct skyscrapers, design and build power stations, and they generally create the modern world with which we are familiar. However, the demands on engineers do not end there. They are often required to be project managers and to administer complex contracts, both in the UK and abroad. In these various roles, engineers or architects often have to deal with disputes, whether with a contractor over certified sums, with an employer about unpaid fees, or with a supplier over substandard materials. In this book the term 'engineer' is used as convenient shorthand for all professionals involved in construction and engineering projects.

The purpose of this book is to serve as the engineer's guide when a dispute does arise. It is intended to be an intensely practical and useful book. It avoids legal jargon and sets out, in straightforward language, how the engineer can avoid disputes, if at all possible, and how to cope with those that cannot be avoided. However, please remember that this book is not giving legal advice. It is merely making suggestions as to how to approach dispute problems. If you do have a specific dispute, then you should consider seeking legal advice. See Chapter 3 for how to do this. Since the authors are not intending to give legal advice, they specifically exclude any liability whatsoever, including for negligence.

This book covers all the forms of dispute resolution that an engineer is likely to encounter:

- litigation (Chapter 4)
- arbitration (Chapter 5)
- adjudication (Chapter 6)
- mediation (Chapter 7)
- expert determination (Chapter 8)
- early neutral evaluation (Chapter 9)
- dispute boards (Chapter 10).

For each type of dispute procedure you will be led, step-by-step, through the process, in a practical way. If you want to do your own research, you will be guided to accessible libraries and websites. If you want to instruct professionals to assist you, you are given contact details with suggestions on how to go about it. If you need to choose between different dispute processes, you are given useful comparisons of the pros and cons of each procedure.

Since the UK engineering profession and construction industry are heavily engaged abroad, there is a separate chapter (Chapter 10) dealing specifically with international dispute resolution procedures, pointing out how these differ from dispute processes used in the UK. That chapter gives particular guidance on the growing use of dispute boards.

Only 10 years ago an engineer faced with a dispute would simply have had to choose between litigation or arbitration. However, in recent years a range of new procedures have become available, many of which offer much cheaper and quicker alternatives. Although processes such as mediation, adjudication and early neutral evaluation are, in theory, simply steps that can be tried en route to a full-blown arbitration or court case, in reality these new procedures generally dispose of the dispute altogether. Mediation, for example, has a success rate generally greater than 70%. Similarly, the vast majority of disputes dealt with by adjudication never proceed to arbitration or litigation; the parties simply accept the adjudicator's decision. The same applies to early neutral evaluation. Thus, one of the most important decisions an engineer may have to make in the course of a project is precisely what strategy to adopt as regards dispute resolution. Should the choice be to opt for mediation, with adjudication as a fallback, and arbitration if all else fails; or would it be better to choose early neutral evaluation and then a possible court case? Alternatively, an expert determination might satisfactorily dispose of a particular technical or financial issue. This book gives sensible, straightforward guidance to any engineer facing such questions.

This book has been written by a team of specialists from Keating Chambers, one of the leading sets of construction and engineering barristers' chambers in the UK. Many of the authors are themselves Chartered Engineers and one is a building surveyor. Their expertise includes civil, electrical, mechanical and chemical engineering. This is not a tome for lawyers; it is a down-to-earth handbook for engineers and other construction professionals, written by specialists who are both engineers and barristers. It is, we believe, unique, and we hope that you find it useful. If, having used it, you have any comments, whether praise or criticism, please let us know at the email address given at the end of Chapter 12. We also have a website at www.keatingchambers.com

Overview of the forms of dispute resolution

Some procedures are finally determinative. Once those procedures have run their course there is a final and binding decision, subject to appeal only where this is permitted. Those procedures are, principally, court litigation, arbitration and expert determination. However, there is a growing range of preliminary procedures which very effectively screen out the vast majority of disputes to which they are applied. These are adjudication, mediation, dispute boards and early neutral evaluation (ENE). This book deals with all of the above procedures, so that the engineer is able to make an informed choice at each stage of the problem.

To enhance the usefulness of each chapter, where appropriate there is a model notice of arbitration, or a mediation position paper, and so on. This means that when a construction professional needs to deal with a dispute this book ought to provide the material necessary for decisive action.

Other than for court litigation, which is, of course, governed by the procedures of the national courts, most other forms of dispute resolution can be easily applied to international projects. Accordingly, this book (Chapter 10) outlines dispute resolution in an international context. Thus, whether working in the UK or running a site in the Middle East, Far East or anywhere else, engineers faced with a dispute problem will find that help is at hand in this book.

The seven forms of dispute resolution
The seven forms of dispute resolution mentioned above are each now described briefly.

Final determination procedures
Court litigation
For the purposes of construction disputes, 'court litigation' means trials in the Technology and Construction Court (TCC). The principal TCC court is in London, but specialist TCC judges also sit in the main UK provincial centres.

If proceedings are commenced in the TCC, the relevant procedures in the Civil Procedure Rules (CPR) must be observed, including the fulfilment of the protocols. There may well be substantial disclosure of documents required of the parties, and technical experts may need to be engaged. This, when taken in conjunction with the involvement of solicitors, barristers and court charges, may mean that court litigation is an expensive procedure.

The parties have to set out their respective cases in detail on paper in their pleadings. Witnesses must produce detailed statements of their evidence, and experts must produce reports. This all adds to the cost. Accordingly, the engineer will, throughout the process, be considering whether it is possible to secure a satisfactory resolution by some other means, such as negotiation or mediation.

Arbitration
Arbitration has the advantage over litigation that it is entirely confidential, so that the parties involved do not have to expose themselves or their dispute to public scrutiny. However, the costs overall are generally similar to those incurred in court litigation because similar procedures are used.

A vast number of construction disputes arise in contracts where arbitration is specified within the contract as the agreed form of dispute resolution. In such circumstances court litigation is generally not an option. However, it is still open to the engineer to seek to dispose of the dispute by some other means, such as mediation or adjudication.

Expert determination

Although little used, the popularity of expert determination is growing as construction professionals realise that it can provide a satisfactory outcome where there is a particular technical issue. For example, if there is a financial issue where both sides would be prepared to accept the view of an independent accountant, a quantity surveying dispute where both would accept the views of an impartial quantity surveyor, or a technical matter, such as whether a power station boiler is up to specification, where both parties would abide by the view of a jointly appointed consulting engineer, then this procedure may well be appropriate.

If the procedure has not been written into the contract it can only be used if both parties agree to it. If it is used, then it is generally only suitable for a single issue, or for a handful of associated issues, of a particular type. Experts are subject to little court control since their decisions are generally not open to appeal. They may adopt an inquisitorial procedure, and are not obliged to refer the results of their inquiries to the parties before making any determination. Accordingly, it is not every case where this procedure is suitable. Nevertheless, if there is a single dispute that is preventing the parties reaching a compromise, this process may be the means of releasing the log jam.

Preliminary determination procedures
Mediation

In the UK, mediation generally means a 'facilitative' process where the mediator helps the parties to make a deal. This should not be confused with an 'evaluative' process (more commonly called 'conciliation' in the UK), where the mediator, at the end of the process, gives an assessment of what the outcome should be if no deal has been done.

Where parties do in fact want an evaluative process, a simple solution is to try mediation first, since this is quicker and cheaper than any evaluative process and, if that fails, to have an ENE (see the following subsection).

The obvious attraction of mediation is that it is reasonably low cost since it generally involves only a one-day meeting, with minimal paperwork beforehand. It can also be set up very quickly; most mediations are arranged within a matter of weeks. The success rate is extremely high, depending on the precise type of dispute and the skill of the particular mediator.

Early neutral evaluation (ENE)

This process involves a preliminary assessment of the likely outcome of the various issues in dispute. The evaluation is designed to serve as a basis for further negotiation and, hopefully, to avoid litigation or arbitration. An independent person is appointed by the parties, and that evaluator expresses an opinion on the merits of the issues raised. The opinion is non-binding, but the parties receive an unbiased evaluation of their relative strengths and guidance as to the likely outcome if they proceed to court or arbitration.

Adjudication

This procedure is undoubtedly the most exciting new development in construction dispute resolution. Statutory adjudication was introduced by the Housing Grants, Construction and Regeneration Act 1996 ('the Act') and came into force in May 1998. It met a real need, securing the cash flow of interim payments to subcontractors and others, and outlawed 'pay-when-paid' clauses except in certain circumstances.

The payment provisions in the Act are coupled with an adjudication procedure which allows for a fast-track determination within 28 days, unless a longer period is agreed. This prevents prevarication by the paying party. In addition, a combination of payment procedures and adjudication machinery has been backed up by a series of robust decisions by the TCC and Court of Appeal judges, which make plain that it is parliament's intention that adjudication decisions should generally be enforced as they are subject to subsequent litigation or arbitration if a party is dissatisfied.

The success of adjudication in the UK is attested by the fact that broadly similar schemes have now been introduced in other common-law jurisdictions, including particularly Australia, New Zealand, Singapore and, soon, Malaysia. In addition, in both Hong Kong and South Africa, important and widely used construction contracts include provision for adjudication. It is even the case that in certain World Bank funded projects the contract terms provide for adjudication, notwithstanding that the projects are based well outside the Commonwealth or any common-law jurisdiction.

Dispute boards/panels

Dispute boards (DBs) involve a procedure whereby a panel of three engineers/lawyers (sometimes just one) is appointed at the outset of a project. The DB visits the project site several times a year and deals with any insipient disputes. This generally avoids a dispute crystallising into an arbitration.

FIDIC (the Fédération Internationale des Ingénieurs-Conseils) has included the DB procedure in its standard forms for some time. Recently, the Paris-based International Chamber of Commerce (ICC) has produced a well-received set of DB rules.

In essence, the DB procedure amounts to serial adjudication. Each time the board makes a decision it is similar to an adjudicator producing a decision, and is, generally, temporarily binding unless either party challenges it by commencing arbitration within a stipulated time limit. If there is no challenge in that way, then the decision of the DB becomes binding.

It will be apparent from this brief survey of the various forms of dispute resolution currently available, all of which are described in this book, that whatever the nature of the dispute, whatever its size, and at whatever point it arises during the project, there is likely to be a particular procedure, or a combination of procedures, that is most suitable for tackling it and disposing of it in the most cost-effective way possible. This book will enable the engineer to make the appropriate decisions to achieve that outcome.

2. Avoiding disputes

Gaynor Chambers

Introduction

Disputes in the construction industry are often lengthy, complex and expensive to resolve. They can also cause long-term damage to the commercial relationships between the parties. However, many disputes could be avoided (or at least contained) by ensuring that a formalised contract is made, which is drafted clearly and fairly and contains provisions for early dispute resolution and effective contract management.

Contractual means of avoiding disputes

There are four basic precautions which contribute to the minimisation of disputes:

- Ensure that the parties enter into a finalised contract before works commence.
- Ensure the scope and quality of the works are clearly defined at the pre-contract stage.
- Ensure the contract terms are fair and clear, and utilise standard forms of contracts wherever possible.
- Ensure that the contract used contains provisions for the early notification of potential disputes and a well-structured dispute resolution clause which is not limited to arbitration/litigation.

The importance of finalising the contract

Finalising the contract is an essential and yet often overlooked step in construction and engineering projects, many of which commence on the basis of letters of intent. While such letters may be necessary in some situations, they can pose a significant risk to the employer and should not be utilised without careful consideration.

Although there are limited occasions where the lack of an agreed and signed contract could operate in the employer's favour, in general the party which has the most to gain (and which is the most likely therefore to delay formalisation) is the contractor. Prior to contract award, the employer's willingness to pay an amount of money is perhaps the main source of the employer's strength in contract negotiations. Once the employer commits to the contractor and authorises the commencement of preliminary works, this advantage is lost and the employer is exposed to an immediate risk of disputes arising as to what was or should have been agreed.

Once the project is underway, sorting out the final form of contract and getting all the relevant parties to physically sign the agreed document are often overlooked in the drive simply to get the job done. However, failure to formalise the parties' relationship has in the past led to the following problems:

- The contractor successfully claiming an entitlement to be paid on a *quantum meruit* basis whilst the employer is unable to counterclaim for delay (see Box 2.1).

Box 2.1: *British Steel Corporation* v. *Cleveland Bridge Engineering Co. Ltd* (1984) All ER 504

In this case the Defendant (CBE) instructed the Plaintiff (BSC) to start manufacturing certain bespoke cast-steel nodes pending the issue of an official form of subcontract. Manufacturing commenced, but the parties were unable to agree on the terms of the subcontract (the main problem being that each company wanted to use its own set of standard terms). The nodes were delivered with some delay due to industrial action and production problems, but still no contract had been concluded. CBE also contended that the nodes had been delivered out of sequence. BSC sued for the price and the court held that it was entitled to be paid a reasonable sum for the nodes on a *quantum meruit* basis. CBE's counterclaim for damages for delay and out-of-sequence delivery was rejected. Without a contract, there was no legal basis for this claim.

- Arguments over the form of contract which the parties actually intended to enter into (see Box 2.2).

Box 2.2: *Butler Machine Tool Co. Ltd* v. *Ex-Cell-O-Corporation* (1979) 1 WLR 401 (CA)

This case concerned a contract for the sale of a machine tool. Following initial negotiations, the seller issued a quotation that gave a price and delivery date of 10 months and stated that the order was subject to the seller's own terms and conditions, which were printed on the back of the order. The seller's terms and conditions included a price variation clause. The buyer responded by issuing an order which stated that the seller was to supply the tool 'on terms and conditions below and overleaf'. These terms and conditions were different from the seller's terms and conditions and, in particular, did not include a price variation clause. There was a tear-off slip at the end of the order which was duly signed and returned by the seller, under cover of a letter stating that the tool would be delivered in accordance with the seller's original quotation. Proceedings ensued in which the sellers

---

sought to take advantage of the price variation clause. The judge at first instance held that the contract had been concluded on the seller's terms and conditions, but the Court of Appeal held that by returning the tear-off slip, they had accepted the buyer's terms and conditions.

- Disputes as to whether or not the letter of intent itself is enforceable or simply an 'agreement to agree', meaning that the parties' respective contractual rights are entirely undefined (see Box 2.3).

Box 2.3
- In *British Steel Corporation* v. *Cleveland Bridge Engineering Co. Ltd* (1984) discussed above, the instruction to commence manufacturing was contained within a letter of intent from CBE which stated its intention to enter into a contract on its standard form of subcontract. The court rejected the argument that BSC had agreed to contract on these terms simply by commencing manufacturing.
- In *Turriff Construction* v. *Regalia Knitting Mills* (1971) 222 EG 169 design work for a construction project was undertaken following the issue of a letter of intent but the project was abandoned before a formal contract was entered into. The court found that the employer was liable to pay the costs of the abortive design work because the letter of intent had given rise to an ancillary contract.

The above list is clearly not exhaustive but serves to illustrate the basic principle of '*caveat* employer' – letters of intent favour the contractor and, notwithstanding the time pressures which affect many contracts, should be avoided wherever possible in favour of a properly executed contract.

Clearly define the scope of the works and quality expected
Disputes generally arise in relation to the following matters:

- The scope of the work – what was actually agreed, and whether or not a particular item or area of the works is a variation or was part of the original scope.
- The contract sum – disputes typically centre on what this covers.
- Quality – whether the workmanship and/or materials are of the required quality.
- Time – whether the contractor or employer are responsible for any delays to the project (and any costs arising out of these delays).
- Payment – or more usually non-payment by the employer to the contractor.
- Unforeseen conditions – which party bears the costs risk?
- Employer's risks and compensation events.

The possibility of lengthy disputes arising in these areas can be minimised by clear and fair contract drafting, a topic which is considered in the following subsection. However, clearly defining the scope and quality of the works in the early stages (i.e. before tender or during the tender negotiations) can assist in preventing disputes. For example, the usual reason why additional time is required is variations (or alleged variations) to the project works.

The scope of work is easier to define when the plans and drawings are complete at the time the contract is negotiated.

Similarly, the potential for disputes as to whether materials meet the required standard can be reduced if:

- recognised standards, such as British Standards, are stipulated where possible
- the particular materials to be used are specified in the contract documents.

Ensuring the contract terms are clear and fair

Research carried out by the Project and Construction Management Group at the University of Birmingham in 1995 discovered the following:

- The use of a clear form of standard contract (in this case the NEC) did not prevent disputes, as disputes happen between people regardless of the contract form adopted.
- However, there were fewer sources of conflict or dispute within the NEC due to its precise drafting. This meant that when an event occurred or an error was exposed, it was clear on the face of the contract which party was responsible for it. The potential for argument was thereby reduced.

These results expose one of the key difficulties in many construction contracts, namely that the contract fails to make plain which party bears the risk of delay or increased expense caused by a particular event.

Plain language can of course assist with this difficulty. However, the potential for dispute can be further minimised by making use of a standard-form contract.

Examples of standard form contracts are listed in Box 2.4.

Box 2.4: Standard forms of contract for construction and engineering projects

- The Joint Contracts Tribunal (JCT) range – for building projects.
- The Institution of Chemical Engineers (IChemE) Model Forms – for process engineering.
- The Joint Institution of Mechanical Engineers/Institution of Electrical Engineers Model Forms MF1–4 – for electrical/mechanical projects.
- NEC Engineering and Construction Contract, 3rd edition.
- The Institution of Civil Engineers (ICE) forms – for civil engineering.

The use of standard-form contracts can help to reduce the potential for disputes in a number of ways.

- Because these forms have been in wide use for a number of years, there is an existing body of case law in relation to the main sets of standard-form contracts which can assist in resolving disputes as to the interpretation of particular clauses. There are also authoritative commentaries which can be referred to (see for example the commentary on the ICE form of contract found in *Keating on Building Contracts*, 7th edition).
- Because of their longstanding use and the fact that they have been revised over time, the standard forms are likely to cover most of the potential dispute scenarios which are likely to arise on a project of the kind for which they are used.
- Because the forms themselves are usually drafted by composite panels which reflect the views of all stakeholders in the contract, the terms are generally fair and recognise the interests and expectations of both parties.
- Because of the above factors, insurers are generally more relaxed when asked to provide insurance for projects which are to be carried out under a recognised standard-form of contract. This means that premiums are lower and the likelihood of a dispute with the insurer, if a claim is made, is reduced.

The use of standard-form contracts can have further incidental benefits for all parties in the construction process.

- Production of tender documents is quicker.
- Tendering contractors can respond more quickly because of their familiarity with the contract form in question.
- The work of the contract administrators is also simplified if they are using a form of which they have prior experience.

It is often the case that substantial amendments are made to standard form conditions of contract. These are usually based on the relevant party (whether employer or contractor) seeking to allocate additional risk to the other. Such amendments should generally be avoided, as they can remove the benefits of using the standard form. They may also have effects which were not anticipated when they were drafted and which may be contrary to the objectives of the party who originally sought the amendment (see for example Box 2.5).

Box 2.5: *Wates Construction* v. *Franthom Property Ltd* (1991) 53 BLR 23 (CA)

In this case the parties had contracted using the JCT Standard Form of Building Contract Without Quantities, which provided that interim payments should be subject to a 5% retention. Clause 30.5.1 of the standard form provided that the employer's interest in the retention money was fiduciary as trustee for the contractor. However, clause 30.5.3, which provided that the retention money

---

was to be kept in a separate and identified bank account, had been deleted prior to signing. The contractor discovered that the money was not being kept separate from the employer's general working capital and asked the court to order that it should be put in a separate account. The Court of Appeal held that, despite the deletion of clause 30.5.3, the employer was obliged to keep the funds in a separate bank account as part of his duties as trustee pursuant to clause 30.5.1.

Ensure the dispute resolution clause is well-structured

The contract should set out clearly what is to take place in the event of a dispute. The dispute resolution clause should ideally provide for an escalating succession of dispute resolution mechanisms in order to resolve the dispute at the earliest opportunity. For example, the following measures could be provided for:

(1) inter-party negotiation
(2) mediation
(3) expert determination
(4) early neutral evaluation (ENE)
(5) adjudication.

The traditional means of dealing with engineering and construction disputes has been via litigation in court or arbitration. Both have proven to be relatively expensive ways for the parties to achieve a detailed final determination of a complex dispute. Not all the measures listed above lead to a determination, and any decision which is reached by expert determination or adjudication is generally only temporarily binding (until one of the parties decides to proceed to arbitration or litigation). In practice, however, these measures have proven highly successful in enabling the parties to move towards the final resolution of their differences without recourse to an arbitrator or the courts.

It is therefore becoming increasingly common for engineering and construction contracts to have tiered dispute resolution clauses. The first tier is usually some form of non-binding 'alternative dispute resolution'. For example, there may be a provision for the formal notification of any matter with which either party is dissatisfied, with the parties then meeting to discuss and seek to resolve the matter. The clause may then go on to provide for adjudication and/or expert determination and/or ENE, with arbitration being the final means of dispute resolution rather than the first.

This approach of setting out a tiered list of procedures has been adopted (since 2005) in the new suite of JCT standard form contracts. For example the Major Project Contract expressly provides at clause 41 for the resolution of disputes by mediation (where the parties agree to this), adjudication or legal proceedings.

The tiered approach was also adopted by the Hong Kong Government's Works Bureau on the Airport Core Programme (ACP) contracts, with the stages being an engineer's decision, mediation, adjudication and ultimately arbitration. The success of the tiered approach is reflected in the fact that 79% of all disputes on the ACP contracts were resolved at the mediation stage. For details see 'Hong Kong Airport Project provides innovative ADR system' by Wall C.J. (1992) *World Arbitration and Mediation Report*, volume 3, number 6, pages 10–153.

The underlying reason for adopting a tiered dispute resolution process is that the non-binding processes are generally cheaper and faster and should therefore be tried first, before the parties incur the expense of the more traditional formalised methods of dispute resolution. It should be borne in mind that the costs of arbitration or litigation extend beyond those of lawyers and experts, particularly as both parties will have to commit the time of the key personnel to the preparation of factual evidence and (eventually) any hearing.

It should be noted again that clarity of drafting is essential (see Box 2.6).

Box 2.6: *Aiton Australia Pty Ltd* v. *Transfield Pty Ltd* [1999] NSWSC 1996

In this Australian case, relatively detailed tiered alternative dispute resolution clauses in a construction contract were held to lack sufficient certainty. This led to the defendant's application to stay the court proceedings (in order to first try the contractual dispute resolution mechanisms) being dismissed. The primary reason why the dispute resolution clauses were deemed to lack certainty was because there were no provisions dealing with the appointment of a further mediator should the mediator the parties originally sought to appoint be unable or unwilling to act, or dealing with the remuneration of the mediator.

Although it is, of course, always open to parties to agree to mediate or have an expert determination or ENE regardless of whether such procedures are mentioned in the contract, experience shows that if these procedures are not expressly included in the dispute resolution clause, neither party is likely to suggest them. One reason for this is the perception that the suggestion of mediation or some other form of dispute resolution is likely to be seen as a reflection of the suggesting party's lack of faith in its case.

Another reason for not suggesting mediation, expert determination or ENE can be the employer's reticence to have matters resolved relatively speedily once a project has been completed and a sum of money is claimed as due to the contractor. As part of the adversarial process, an employer may wish to delay matters and make the procedure as costly as possible in an attempt to force the contractor into settling on terms which are relatively advantageous to the employer. This is, however, a dangerous tactic which may well backfire: contractors' post-completion claims relatively rarely fail in their entirety, and once some monies are recovered it is the employer rather than the contractor who will be most likely to pay the costs of the dispute.

It is therefore in all parties' interests to enter into a contract in which alternative dispute resolution procedures are expressly required by the contract, so that the parties can seek to resolve any dispute as rapidly and cost-effectively as possible.

Effective contract management

Once the project is underway, good contract management will help avoid or minimise the potential for disputes. Following the early notification of disputes it is important to keep thorough records. These records can then be used to stop a dispute developing and ensure that the negotiations that take place are based on fact and not merely on conjecture. (See also the discussion in Chapter 10.)

In the majority of cases, disputes and claims which have been building up over the course of a project will be put forward as a claim at the end of the project. This is understandable given that:

- during the course of the project the parties are more concerned to get the job done than with claims related matters, and
- whatever views are expressed during the course of the project, there usually remains some hope of resolving all outstanding claims as part of the final account process.

However, this can mean that the claim is formulated by someone who was not involved throughout the project. The party seeking to claim might instruct external lawyers or claims consultants, who are unlikely to be called in until the stage where things have begun to go seriously wrong and the project is in danger of running at a loss (contractor) or going over budget (employer). Even where a contractor relies on its own in-house lawyers or quantity surveyors, these people may not have been involved from the outset of the claims. It is not unusual for a contractor to call in a senior project manager or other figure when a project is in trouble, who will then be responsible for getting matters back on track and pursuing any necessary claims.

The problem of the people drafting claims lacking contemporaneous knowledge can be ameliorated to some extent if either or both parties is able to produce unequivocal records showing the true position at the time of the events in question. For example, if it is claimed that the progress of the works has been affected by particularly adverse weather conditions, site diaries and dated and labelled photographs can both provide good evidence of the actual delay caused. Too often, the only evidence relied upon is meteorological records, which go only to show the potential for delay and disruption due to adverse weather (rather than being evidence of the actual delay and disruption experienced).

Finally, it is essential to ensure that these records and contemporaneous documents are preserved in an orderly and accessible manner after the project has ended. For example, in preparing a delay and disruption claim, witnesses often bemoan that although they cannot remember the precise detail of costs and time expended as a result of a particular event, records were kept which have now been lost. Or a witness may state that he cannot recall exactly what happened in relation to a particular delay event referred to in the correspondence but that he would be able to if he had his site diary, which was left in the site office when he left the project (and has not been seen since).

Accordingly, at the end of a project where there is likely to be a dispute, it is in the interests of both parties to ensure that key personnel on site are made aware of the arrangements for record keeping and asked to bring their own records, such as site diaries and internal memos, to the attention of the designated archivist.

3. When disputes arise

Paul Buckingham, Samuel Townend and Jonathan Selby

Overview

Whatever form of dispute resolution is adopted, there has to be a dispute to resolve. Most people know what a dispute is when one arises. However, a large body of case law has developed on the meaning of the word 'dispute'. In *Amec Civil Engineering* v. *Secretary of State for Transport* [2004] EWHC 2339 (TCC) Jackson J summarised all the relevant case law and, at paragraph 68 of his judgment, identified seven propositions, as follows.

1 The word 'dispute' should be given its normal meaning. It does not have some special or unusual meaning conferred upon it by lawyers.

2 Despite the simple meaning of the word 'dispute', there has been much litigation over the years as to whether or not disputes existed in particular situations. This litigation has not generated any hard-edged legal rules as to what is or is not a dispute. However, the accumulating judicial decisions have produced helpful guidance.

3 The mere fact that one party (whom I shall call 'the claimant') notifies the other party (whom I shall call 'the respondent') of a claim does not automatically and immediately give rise to a dispute. It is clear, both as a matter of language and from judicial decisions, that a dispute does not arise unless and until it emerges that the claim is not admitted.

4 The circumstances from which it may emerge that a claim is not admitted are Protean. For example, there may be an express rejection of the claim. There may be discussions between the parties from which objectively it is to be inferred that the claim is not admitted. The respondent may prevaricate, thus giving rise to the inference that he does not admit the claim. The respondent may simply remain silent for a period of time, thus giving rise to the same inference.

5 The period of time for which a respondent may remain silent before a dispute is to be inferred depends heavily upon the facts of the case and the contractual structure. Where the gist of the claim is well known and it is obviously controversial, a very short period of silence may suffice to give rise to this inference. Where the claim is notified to some agent of the respondent who has a legal duty to consider the claim independently and then give a considered

response, a longer period of time may be required before it can be inferred that mere silence gives rise to a dispute.

6 If the claimant imposes upon the respondent a deadline for responding to the claim, that deadline does not have the automatic effect of curtailing what would otherwise be a reasonable time for responding. On the other hand, a stated deadline and the reasons for its imposition may be relevant factors when the court comes to consider what is a reasonable time for responding.

7 If the claim as presented by the claimant is so nebulous and ill-defined that the respondent cannot sensibly respond to it, neither silence by the respondent nor even an express non-admission is likely to give rise to a dispute for the purposes of arbitration or adjudication.

These propositions have been generally endorsed by the Court of Appeal in *Collins Contractors (Contractors) Ltd* v. *Baltic Quay Management (1994) Ltd* [2005] BLR 63 and in the *Amec* case itself [2005] 1 BLR 227. What is clear from the propositions is that, for a dispute to arise at all, a claim has to be made in the first place.

This chapter therefore looks at:

- how to initiate a claim
- defending a claim
- instructing lawyers, and
- direct access schemes.

Initiating a claim
Choosing the dispute procedure
When selecting the procedure to adopt to resolve a dispute, the first point of reference should be any contract between the parties to the dispute. This is for two reasons. The first is that the contract may have clauses which stipulate how disputes are to be resolved. The second is that the contract may be one to which the Housing Grants, Construction and Regeneration Act 1996 ('the Act') applies. If it is, each party will also have the right to refer their dispute to adjudication – even if the contract itself contains no express provision for adjudication and even if one of the parties does not want to refer the dispute to adjudication. Adjudication is discussed more fully in Chapter 6.

There are numerous ways in which the contract may stipulate how disputes are to be resolved. By way of example:

- ICE contracts require disputes to be referred to the Engineer for a decision before more formal methods of dispute resolution are adopted.
- Some contracts require meetings of senior executives before more formal methods of dispute resolution are adopted. Similarly, they may have 'mediation clauses' which require the parties to attempt to resolve the dispute through mediation before they can commence proceedings. In such circumstances, the courts may often prevent court proceedings from continuing unless and until a mediation has taken place (see *Cable & Wireless plc* v. *IBM United Kingdom plc* [2003] BLR 89).

(Mediation is discussed in Chapter 7.) However, such clauses ought not to prevent a party from referring a dispute to adjudication – even if no mediation has taken place before the adjudication is commenced (see *R.G. Carter Ltd* v. *Edmund Nuttall Ltd*, unreported, 21 June 2000).

- Whether or not the Act applies, the contract may also expressly permit parties to refer disputes to adjudication. Where the contract contains such clauses, their terms need to be considered carefully as they will often detail matters such as how the adjudicator should be appointed, the procedure which will be adopted in the adjudication, and whether a particular party will be liable for the costs of the adjudication.
- The contract may have an arbitration clause. In such circumstances, claims cannot be pursued in court – see section 9 of the Arbitration Act 1996. Arbitration is discussed in Chapter 5.
- The contract may have a jurisdiction clause. This will determine what national courts the dispute can be resolved in.

The contract may also have a choice of law clause, especially if it has an 'international flavour' (for example, because it relates to a project in the middle of the sea or because the parties are from different countries). This will determine the law by which the dispute is governed – and may therefore determine which lawyers are instructed.

However, the contract should not be the only factor which determines the method of dispute resolution to be used. Other factors which may be of relevance include:

- Confidentiality – the nature of the project may be such that the parties want to keep their dispute confidential. If confidentiality is important, court proceedings should be avoided because they are generally open to the public.
- Working relationships – although a dispute may have arisen between the parties, it still may be desirable for the dispute to be resolved on amicable terms to protect either future trading relations or existing relations (for example, because the project is not yet complete). If a working relationship needs to be preserved, the parties should consider mediation (discussed in Chapter 7) or early neutral evaluation (discussed in Chapter 9).
- The need for a speedy resolution – if the dispute has to be resolved quickly, for example, because it is holding up the progress of the project or because there is an urgent need for the money, the parties should consider adjudication (discussed in Chapter 6) or early neutral evaluation (discussed in Chapter 9).
- Limitation – a party's right to pursue the claim may be barred if arbitration or court proceedings are not commenced within a specified time limit. That time limit may be specified in the contract (for example, some contracts contain clauses which provide that claims must be notified to the other party within a certain time) or by statute. In the context of English law, the main statute is the Limitation Act 1980 which provides that claims for breach of contract must be commenced within 6 years from the date of the breach unless the contract is executed as a deed, in which case the claim must be commenced within 12 years.

- Costs/proportionality – the value of the claim and the cost of pursuing it ought also to be considered. Lengthier processes such as litigation (discussed in Chapter 4) and arbitration (discussed in Chapter 5) are generally more expensive than shorter processes such as adjudication (discussed in Chapter 6), mediation (discussed in Chapter 7) and expert determination (discussed in Chapter 8).
- Complexity – if the dispute is technically complex, it may be better resolved by a decision-maker with the appropriate expertise. In such circumstances, the parties should consider a method of dispute resolution such as expert determination (discussed in Chapter 8) or arbitration with a specialist arbitrator (discussed in Chapter 5). Here, the parties can agree (or seek the appointment of) a decision-maker with the appropriate expertise.

Making the claim

Not only is the contract important in deciding which method of dispute resolution to adopt, it should also be consulted before a claim is made. Some contracts prescribe the manner in which the claim is first to be made and identify the particulars and type of information which need to be provided in the initial claim document. Sometimes, the contract may simply require some basic information (such as names and addresses and the value of the claim). However, some contracts contain detailed requirements as to the kinds of information which have to be provided and, for example, can require supporting documentation to be submitted with a letter of claim. These requirements should be complied with because, if they are not, a party's right to pursue the dispute further may be seriously prejudiced. For example, because the contract requirements have not been complied with, it may be held that a dispute has not yet arisen which is capable of reference to adjudication.

Generally, any claim should be started by sending a letter of claim. Not only is this a prerequisite to the formulation of a dispute (see above), but it is also required as part of the pre-action protocols which have to be complied with in advance of the commencement of court proceedings. Pre-action protocols are discussed in Chapter 4.

Irrespective of what the contract provides, it is generally good practice to provide as much relevant information as possible with a letter of claim, including supporting documents and any expert reports which are available. The more relevant information which is provided, the more likely it will be that a claim is taken seriously. It is also always worth concluding the letter of claim by suggesting possible methods of dispute resolution. This again shows that the claimant is serious about the dispute.

A sample letter of claim is set out in Box 3.1. (A letter of claim for more complex circumstances may be found in Chapter 4.)

Defending a claim

Deadlines

The most important point to remember about defending a claim is that there is almost always a deadline within which the defence or response must be served on the other party. These deadlines can be tight. For

---

Box 3.1: Sample letter of claim

Dear Sir

Re: Defective Air Conditioning

We write in relation to the air conditioning which you installed at the new office building at 10–25 Smith Street, Smithville.

By clause 15 of the specification, the air conditioning was supposed to maintain the temperature of the building at 10 °C throughout the day.

However, the air conditioning does not achieve this target and instead the temperature in the building is 15 °C. As is confirmed by the report of Professor Jones, Consulting Engineer, this is due to a fault in the air handling units, which he considers need to be replaced.

Given your refusal to replace the air handling units yourselves, we had to engage an alternative contractor (Aircon Ltd) to install new units instead. The total cost of this work was £150,000 plus VAT and a copy of Aircon's contract and final account is included for your information.

Please therefore pay us £150,000 plus VAT within 14 days.

Otherwise, we will be left with no other option than to pursue this matter through more formal means. In this regard, we note that clause 72 of the Contract Conditions entitles us to commence adjudication or arbitration proceedings to recover this money. Whilst we are prepared to use such methods of dispute resolution if necessary, we are willing to meet with you on a without prejudice basis or in a mediation to see if this matter can be resolved on a more amicable basis.

Yours etc.

---

example, in adjudication the responding party can have as little as 7 days to respond and in court proceedings the defendant will have 14 to 28 days.

Given the nature of such deadlines, it is always important to act as soon as possible once the claim is received. If it is not possible to respond within the appropriate deadline, the responding party should consider seeking an extension of time. An extension of time can be sought either by agreement with the claimant or by applying to the tribunal which is resolving the dispute (e.g. the court, arbitrator or adjudicator).

The principles which apply to making a claim apply equally to defending a claim. The responding party should obtain as much information as possible in relation to the claim and see how best it can be defended. Not only may there be good arguments in relation to the substantive dispute on which to base a defence, the responding party may find technical issues that would be helpful for successfully defending the claim in its entirety or, at the very least, in stalling it. Therefore, the responding party should not only consider the substantive issues, it should also consider issues such as:

- Would the adjudication/arbitration be taking place without juris-diction? If so, any decision reached would be unenforceable.
- Are there any grounds upon which court proceedings can be stayed? If there are, this could stall the proceedings and compel the claimant to commence proceedings in another (potentially undesirable) forum.
- Does the contract contain exclusion clauses which preclude an otherwise valid claim, or has the claim been made too late? Lawyers may need to be instructed to consider this.

In addressing the substantive issues, a respondent should consider the following:

- Has the claimant properly set out the facts? The defence or response should correct any relevant factual inaccuracies.
- What documents are available to contradict the claimant or to support the respondent's arguments?
- Are the relevant people who were involved in the actions which have given rise to the dispute (for example, the agreement of the contract documents or the carrying out of the works) available to assist? If they are, an account of the facts should be obtained from them so that as full a response as possible can be provided.
- Could an expert provide any useful input? If so, an expert with the appropriate qualifications should be commissioned to prepare a report.

Once all the technical and substantive points have been considered, the appropriate response can be formulated and served within the relevant deadline.

Instructing lawyers

The vast majority of disputes arising under construction and engineering projects are dealt with at a project level. In some cases, disputes might be resolved by the intervention of the project manager. However, where claims are of significant value, raise complex issues, or depend upon contractual interpretation, every party should take proper professional advice to help resolve the dispute. That means consulting a lawyer.

There are two main categories of lawyer in England and Wales: solici-tors and barristers. Although the differences between the two professions has diminished considerably over recent years, as a general rule barristers act as advocates, whether in court or arbitration, whereas solicitors provide a wider range of services to the public (advising on non-contentious issues, such as drafting of contracts). A solicitor will often therefore be the first port of call for any party when a dispute arises. However, the rules governing the legal profession have been extended and in appropriate circumstances it is now also possible to instruct a barrister directly to carry out legal work (see the following section – 'Direct access schemes').

Whether a party chooses to instruct a solicitor or barrister, the factors to be considered are similar, and in many ways they are identical to those that a commercial organisation would consider when appointing any professional adviser.

Choosing a lawyer

All lawyers have different qualities, and the key to a successful relationship is selecting a firm with the right qualities for the particular dispute and with which the instructing party feels that it can work effectively and efficiently. In choosing a firm, the following points are important:

- experience
- reputation
- value and complexity of the claim
- resources required and those available
- location.

The importance of location as a factor should not be underestimated. In complicated disputes, regular meetings will be needed. In some cases it might be appropriate to instruct a firm local to the project, where many of the witnesses and personnel are based. In other cases, an office close to the party's head office is more convenient. For international disputes, a London-based firm might be more suitable.

It is also important to be clear about who will have day-to-day responsibility for the conduct of the dispute. Do not be afraid to ask whether this will be a partner in the firm or an assistant solicitor, and if the latter confirm the individual's level of seniority and experience. The success of a party in a dispute is more dependent upon the individual lawyers running the dispute than the reputation of the firm as a whole.

Fees

For dispute work, solicitors traditionally charged their fees based on an hourly rate whereas barristers charged on a lump sum (brief fee) basis. Nowadays, there is much more flexibility in fee structures and charging regimes. The most common options are:

- Hourly rates – where lawyers charge for the time spent working on a matter based on a range of hourly rates depending upon the seniority and experience of each individual lawyer. This mechanism has the advantage of transparency, with a party only being charged for the time actually worked on their matter. The downside is that it is difficult to control costs, and legal fees can build rapidly in a complex case.
- Fixed fees – which are becoming more common, although they are really only appropriate where the nature and scope of the dispute is well defined and there is more certainty. For complex construction disputes, many law firms would be reluctant to agree to a fixed fee given the uncertainties involved.

- Capped fees – which are quite common, and provide a compromise between cost transparency and the degree of certainty as to the ultimate cost.
- Contingency or success fees – which are much more prevalent. Although this fee structure tends to be more appropriate for certain types of litigation work, such as personal injury, it is being increasingly encountered in construction disputes.

Whatever the fee structure agreed, it is also important to be clear about what other costs there will be in addition to those of the lawyers. This can include costs such as:

- court fees
- tribunal's fees
- expert witnesses
- factual witnesses
- document production costs
- travel costs.

Even if fees are being charged on an hourly rate, a party should always ask for a cost estimate for the conduct of the dispute and ensure that it is updated regularly, so that costs are monitored and budgets adjusted as appropriate. It is also sensible to agree to monthly billing or stage payments, so that both parties can monitor the rate at which charges are accumulating and address any unexpected items as they arise.

Agree lines of communication
Conducting a large piece of complex litigation over a period of 1–2 years is in itself a significant project for any party and needs careful management. This will ensure that not only are costs kept to a minimum, but also that the dispute is conducted quickly and efficiently, thereby minimising costs and maximising recovery. For a large dispute, a single individual should be identified and appointed as the point of contact within the client organisation. That individual should have sufficient seniority to make decisions on a day-to-day basis relating to the conduct of the dispute, and also have a sufficient understanding of the case to be able to provide guidance and answer questions that arise. A project manager familiar with both the implementation of the project and the development of the dispute is often an ideal choice, although they might not always be available at the end of a project when moving on to a new project.

A party should also think carefully about the level of control it wants. An experienced law firm is perfectly capable of conducting almost the entirety of a dispute, and can do so with little input from a client save for key strategic decisions. Other clients may wish to review and approve all letters sent to the opposing party and be copied in on all correspondence, so that they can monitor the progress of the dispute. Whilst that level of involvement is often helpful, there are obvious time and cost implications. The key is therefore for the client to build up a good working relationship with a law firm to ensure that they are kept as informed as is necessary, but without being unduly burdened with all the day-to-day issues that necessarily arise in a complex dispute.

Direct access schemes
What is direct access?
Direct access is a scheme under which a member of the public or any organisation can consult a barrister directly. It used to be the case that a client had to consult a solicitor or other recognised professional, who would then appoint a barrister. In these circumstances, if a barrister's advice was needed, both solicitor and barrister had to be paid for it. The direct access scheme offers the opportunity to cut out the middleman and save costs.

There are two systems under the direct access scheme: public access and licensed access. Public access allows an individual or a non-solicitor intermediary to contact a barrister directly. Licensed access allows organisations and individuals that have been granted licenses by the Bar Council to access a barrister directly. Licensed access is the 'fast track' version of the two direct access schemes because the formalities, which must be complied with by the client before a barrister's advice can be sought and given, are less onerous.

In both systems of direct access there are certain restrictions on what a barrister may do during the conduct of a case. A barrister cannot do some of the things which a solicitor can do – for example, a barrister may not conduct a course of correspondence with the other party. A client must be aware of this, particularly because it means that, in the absence of a solicitor who would normally control and execute these aspects of the case, the client will be responsible (under the guidance of the barrister) for doing the things a barrister cannot do. This may be a relevant consideration as to the decision of whether the case is one suitable for the instruction of a barrister but without a solicitor.

What are the advantages for clients of using the direct access scheme?
The major advantage of the direct access scheme is that a client saves the cost of the fees he would otherwise have incurred in instructing a solicitor. The only legal fees payable are those for the barrister. Other advantages include the following:

- It allows the client a greater opportunity to manage their own case, under the guidance of the barrister.
- The client is also able to directly choose his own barrister (as opposed to relying on the solicitor to recommend or select a particular barrister or chambers), thereby potentially affording more consumer choice.

What types of cases are suited to the scheme?
A client seeking the services of a barrister will find that all the services barristers normally perform will be available. These include:

- giving legal advice
- drafting documents
- assisting in the preparation of documents to be used in court

- advocacy in court
- conducting negotiations.

Examples of cases in which a barrister might accept direct access instructions include:

- advice on discrete points, such as interpretation of payment, termination and insurance provisions in ongoing or completed construction and engineering contracts
- help with a negotiation between parties to an engineering contract
- assistance in adjudication or expert determination provided as a method of dispute resolution in the contract.

In most categories of cases, direct instructions to a barrister might be a good starting point. However, the cases in which a solicitor may not be needed at all are those of lesser factual complexity and where there is unlikely to be a need for much extra investigation or gathering of evidence. If a case is complicated or would involve a lot of paperwork and gathering of evidence, the client's needs would probably be better served by having both a solicitor and a barrister involved in the case. If the barrister approached by the client believes this to be the case, the client will be informed that the case is unsuitable for direct access.

There are certain practical aspects of a case which a barrister is not permitted to deal with. This is something which public access clients should consider very carefully. It means that the client will be responsible for much of the administration of the case, and must be prepared to devote time and money to doing what is required. The main things a barrister cannot do are:

- undertake the management of the case (this means the barrister cannot undertake day-to-day matters, such as organising production of statements or collection of evidence)
- conduct litigation (this means the barrister cannot conduct a course of correspondence with an opposing party, although the barrister may draft a letter for the client to send to another person)
- investigate or collect evidence for use in court (this means, for example, the barrister cannot initiate contact with a potential witness, but may help to finalise witness statements based on the information provided by the witness)
- instruct an expert witness or other person on behalf of the client, or accept personal liability for paying any such person (although the barrister may advise the client on the need and choice of a suitable expert)
- receive or handle client money.

In some circumstances, it may be that the client's needs or the interests of justice would be better served by also having a solicitor. This might happen, for example, where the case is of high value and complexity. If this is the case, the barrister is under a professional duty to refuse to do the case on a direct access basis and will inform the client of the need for a solicitor. If a barrister accepts a case on a direct access basis and it subsequently becomes clear that a solicitor is required, the barrister will also inform the client of this.

If this happens, the client may continue to use the same barrister as one half of their legal team, as long as a solicitor is also engaged (the relationship between the parties would then become the traditional relationship, whereby the solicitor and not the lay client generally deals with the barrister).

Types of direct access
Licensed access
Licensed access has replaced 'BarDirect' and 'Direct Professional Access' as the means by which members of certain professional bodies may instruct barristers directly. It allows those with the designated qualifications to instruct barristers directly for advisory and advocacy work and without any significant formalities having to be complied with.

A client (organisation or individual professional) wishing to take advantage of this scheme must apply to the Bar Council for a license. Application forms, together with the Licensed Access Guidance and Licensed Access Recognition Regulations, can be downloaded from the Bar Council website at www.barcouncil.org.uk

This license will then enable the client to access a barrister directly. It is a very user-friendly system: there is little administration involved in the initial contact with the barrister, there is a wide pool of barristers available to the client (unlike with the public access scheme, there are no restrictions under the licensed access scheme as to the qualifications a barrister must hold), and all types of cases can be conducted. The practicalities are limited to procuring the license and supplying it to the barrister's clerk.

A list of organisations which have already been granted a licence can be found on the Bar Council website in the First Schedule to the Licensed Access Recognition Rules. Part IV covers the engineers' organisations which already hold licences. Relevantly, they include:

* the Institution of Chemical Engineers
* the Institution of Civil Engineering Surveyors
* the Institution of Civil Engineers
* the Institution of Electrical Engineers
* the Institution of Mechanical Engineers
* the Institution of Structural Engineers.

Public access
This is the system by which a member of the public is able to consult a barrister directly. Under the scheme, a barrister may accept instructions either from a member of the public or from a non-solicitor intermediary acting on behalf of a member of the public. There are certain limitations as regards the type of work that a barrister may do under this scheme.

As a general rule, a barrister may only accept public access work if he or she:

(1) has been practicing as a barrister for 3 years
(2) has undertaken a training course on direct access, and

(3) has notified the relevant department of the Bar Council of the intention to take on such work.

There is an exception to this: the Bar Council can in certain circumstances waive the first two requirements. This might happen if, for example, the applicant is a former solicitor or can demonstrate experience in an environment where public access to clients has been common.

In practice, these restrictions mean that only those barristers with sufficient experience are able to undertake public access work. However, some barristers who are technically able to do such work choose not to. A barrister is entitled to refuse to conduct a case under the public access scheme, but may not refuse to do advocacy work on a public access basis save on legitimate grounds. A list of some barristers who undertake public access work is available on the Bar Council website.

Even if the barrister is qualified, there are restrictions on public access based on the content of the case. By the rules of public access, a barrister cannot agree to work on a public access basis if the case is:

- a criminal matter (except for certain appeals, and advisory work in connection with proceedings not yet commenced, when public access work may be undertaken)
- a family matter (except certain appeals, and advisory work and drafting in connection with proceedings not yet commenced, when public access work may be undertaken)
- an immigration matter.

If a case falls into any one of these categories, the barrister will advise the client that the case cannot proceed on a public access basis and that a solicitor must be contacted.

Typical arrangements with a barrister under either of the direct access schemes

The initial contact with a barrister will be the barrister's clerk. After receiving the initial details of the case, it is quite common that the barrister will arrange to have a short discussion with the client. This will be solely to determine whether or not the case is suitable for the direct access scheme, and the barrister will inform the client in advance whether or not payment will be required for this meeting. If the barrister decides to accept the case on a direct access basis, a further conference may need to be arranged to discuss the details of the case further. Once a barrister accepts a direct access case, the client will be sent a client-care letter. This letter explains the terms upon which the case can be accepted. Once the work has been completed, the barrister will inform the client.

Barristers' clerks set and agree the barristers' fees. In many direct access cases, especially public access cases, the barrister will be able to offer a fixed fee arrangement. However, if the case is more complex, or if the barrister so chooses, an hourly rate may be offered. It is also possible that the barrister may provide that work done on the case will be released to the client only once payment (or a percentage of the total payment) has been received.

Whether under the direct access scheme or under the more traditional arrangement, clients should note that there may be times when a barrister is unavailable to the client, particularly as the barrister will have times when they are in court for several days at a time. There may also be times when a barrister's professional commitments clash, so the barrister cannot guarantee to be always available to do the work required. However, the barrister and clerk will always do their best to keep the client informed of any potential difficulties with the barrister's availability, and will try to help if such a problem occurs, for example by recommending another barrister.

LEEDS ST CAR PARK

date issued 20/03/2018

151   this ticket is valid only on date of issue.

CAR PARK CLOSES AT 6.30pm

£3.00

THANK YOU

please display this ticket on your dashboard

Vehicles and their contents are left in this parking place at their owners' risk, Harparks Limited will not be responsible as Bailees or otherwise for loss or damage to any vehicle or its contents.

Harparks Ltd VAT No: 741400476

4. Litigation

Finola O'Farrell, QC

Introduction

Litigation is a public adversarial contest in a court of law for the purpose of enforcing rights and seeking remedies. Once a dispute has been referred to the court, the court has the power to require the parties to follow procedural rules, to compel the production of evidence and to make a binding and enforceable decision.

The reputation of litigation as slow and expensive is disappearing. Cases are actively managed by the court and new technology is employed for efficient use of resources. On 26th April 1999, the Civil Procedure Rules (CPR) came into force, the culmination of a wide-ranging review of court proceedings and root and branch reform of the system instigated by Lord Woolf. The overriding objective of the CPR is to ensure that disputes are dealt with expeditiously, fairly and at a cost proportionate to the size and nature of the case (CPR Part 1.1).

The parties should always explore other forms of dispute resolution before resorting to court proceedings in order to save costs and valuable time. However, litigation can be the appropriate choice in certain circumstances, such as:

- where difficult points of law are involved
- a test case – where there are a number of similar disputes and a clear legal precedent is required
- multi-party disputes – where there are a number of claimants or defendants or where the defendants wish to join others to the proceedings and there is no provision for joinder in any alternative dispute resolution (ADR) procedures
- where there is little or no cooperation and trust between the parties so that management by coercion and speedy enforcement might be required
- where the main remedy sought is an injunction
- where there is no arbitration or other ADR agreement.

The Technology and Construction Court system

Technology and Construction Court (TCC) claims are claims which involve technically complex issues or are otherwise appropriate for trial by a TCC judge (CPR Part 60.1). Most engineering disputes will fall into the category of TCC claims.

TCC proceedings can be brought in the High Court or a county court. There is no strict demarcation but the general rule of thumb is that cases

should be worth at least £50,000 to be brought in the High Court (paragraph 1.3.6 of the *Technology and Construction Court Guide* ('the TCC Guide'); CPR section 2C, page 287).

When a claim is made in or transferred to the TCC, the court will assign the case to a named TCC judge who will have primary responsibility for case management of the claim, including, where possible, the trial. TCC cases started in the High Court in London are classified as 'HCJ' (managed and tried by a High Court judge) or 'SCJ' (managed and tried by a senior circuit judge). If a particular classification is sought, the claimant should write to the TCC when proceedings are issued, setting out the reasons for the requested classification by reference to the following factors:

- size and complexity of the case
- difficult points of law
- amount of money in dispute
- public importance of the dispute
- international element of the dispute.

Pre-action protocols

Pre-action protocols are codes of practice that require parties to exchange information regarding their disputes and to explore the possibility of settlement prior to proceedings. The purpose of the pre-action protocols is to encourage an early exchange of information, to promote early settlements and, if no settlement proves possible, to lay the ground for the efficient conduct of proceedings.

The Pre-Action for Protocol Construction and Engineering Disputes ('the Pre-Action Protocol') applies to all engineering claims in the TCC (CPR section 2C-38). It is mandatory save where the proceedings concern the enforcement of an adjudication award, a claim for an injunction, a summary judgment application or where the same issues have already been the subject of a formal alternative dispute resolution procedure (CPR sections 2C-39 and 40). If there is a limitation difficulty, the claimant should commence proceedings without complying with the protocol and seek directions from the court.

The requirements of the Pre-Action Protocol (CPR section 5C) are as follows:

(1) The claimant sends a letter of claim to each proposed defendant (section 3).
(2) The defendants acknowledge the letter of claim within 14 days of receipt (section 4.1).
(3) The defendants send a letter of response to the claimant within 28 days from receipt of the letter of claim or such other period as the parties may reasonably agree (up to a maximum of 4 months) (section 4.3).
(4) The claimant sends to the defendants a letter of response to any counterclaim within 28 days from receipt of the letter of response from the defendants or such other period as the parties may reasonably agree (up to a maximum of 4 months) (section 4.4).
(5) The parties meet as soon as possible after the above exchange of letters to consider whether settlement is possible, whether ADR is

appropriate and, if litigation is inevitable, the best way of conducting the litigation (such as agreements on disclosure and expert evidence). Such meetings are deemed to be 'without prejudice', i.e. the parties can disclose to the court the fact that such meetings took place, the dates and the attendees but are not permitted to disclose what was said (section 5).

The letter of claim must comply with section 3 of the Pre-Action Protocol. A model letter of claim is set out in Box 4.1.

Box 4.1: Model letter of claim

To: [**Full name and address of each proposed defendant**]

Dear Sir

NEW DELHI POWER STATION PROJECT – Letter of claim served in accordance with the TCC Pre-Action Protocol

1. We are solicitors instructed by the Bavarian Power Company Ltd of [**Full name and address of the claimant**], the contractor engaged by your client (New Delhi Electricity Ltd) to supply, install and commission a new 240 megawatt generator in your client's existing power station.

Clear summary of the facts on which each claim is based

2. The Contract between the parties is an amended version of the MF/1 Model Form of Contract for the supply of electrical or mechanical plant, with erection, produced by the Institution of Electrical Engineers and the Institution of Mechanical Engineers.
3. The works were commenced on 1st April 2003 and carried out in accordance with the Contract. The Time for Completion within the meaning of clause 32 was 12 months (i.e. by 1st April 2004) but delays occurred and the Taking Over Certificate was not issued in respect of the works until 1st April 2005.
4. The said delay was caused by numerous and late variations instructed by your client.
5. On 15th May 2005 our client submitted an application for an extension of time of 12 months and additional payment in the sum of £1million, together with full details of the said claims.
6. Wrongfully and in breach of contract, the Engineer failed to grant any extension of time or to certify any additional sums due to our client and your client has failed to pay any of the sums claimed.
7. Clause 52 of the Contract provides for any disputes between the parties to be determined by the High Court of England and Wales.

Basis of the claims made

8. Attached to this letter are three schedules of the claims:

   - Schedule 1 – Extensions of Time – identifying the key events causing delay, including relevant contractual provisions relied on, the period of delay and delaying effect on the completion date.
   - Schedule 2 – Variations – including for each claim a brief summary of the facts relied on, the relevant contractual provisions and the sum claimed, valued in accordance with clause 27.
   - Schedule 3 – Claims for Additional Costs – including for each claim a brief summary of the facts relied on, the relevant contractual provisions, details of notification given under clause 41 and the sum claimed.

Nature of relief claimed

9. Our client seeks against your client an extension of the time for completion of 12 months and the sum of £1 million as sums due under the Contract and/or as damages. Full details of the damages claimed are set out in the schedules of claim referred to above.

Experts

10. We have instructed the following experts on whose evidence we intend to rely:

    - Teresa White – programming and planning of [**address**]
    - John Smith – electrical engineering of [**address**]
    - Harriet Black – mechanical engineering of [**address**]

11. You are required to acknowledge this letter within 14 days and to provide a response within 28 days.

Yours etc.

The response from the defendants must contain the following information (see section 4 of the Pre-Action Protocol):

(1) Identification of any jurisdiction objection.
(2) Summary of the facts agreed and disagreed, including the basis for any disagreement.
(3) The claims that are accepted and those that are rejected, stating the basis for such rejection.
(4) Response to the claim for damages and the basis for any alternative valuation.
(5) Brief details of any counterclaim.

(6) Names of any experts instructed on whose evidence the defendants intend to rely, identifying the issues to which such evidence will be directed.

The court is concerned with substance, rather than form, when deciding whether or not the Pre-Action Protocol has been followed. If a party fails to comply with the protocol, the court can stay the proceedings to allow the parties to comply or can require the party in default to pay money into court (CPR part 3.1; paragraph 2.6 of the TCC Guide: 2C-43).

The costs of complying with the Pre-Action Protocol can be recovered in subsequent litigation if they can be shown to be incidental to the proceedings within the meaning of section 51 of the Supreme Court Act 1981 but, in the absence of agreement or exceptional circumstances, will not be recoverable if a settlement is achieved or claims abandoned prior to the commencement of proceedings (see *McGlinn* v. *Waltham Contractors Ltd* (2005) CILL 2264 (TCC)).

Commencement of proceedings
Claim form
Legal proceedings are commenced by the issue of a claim form:

- Form N1 is used for part 7 claims (this is the most usual form for engineering claims)
- Form N208 is used for part 8 claims (where there is no substantial dispute of fact, e.g. where the dispute turns on the construction of the contract)
- Form N8 is used for arbitration claims (e.g. appeals from an arbitration award).

The claim form (see Box 4.2) must be served within 4 months of issue by the court and should contain the following information (CPR Part 16.2):

- a concise statement of the nature of the claim
- the remedy that the claimant seeks
- the value of the claim
- verification by a statement of truth.

Statements of case
The particulars of claim must be contained in or served with the claim form or served within 14 days of the claim form (CPR Part 7.4).

The requirements of the particulars of claim are set out in CPR Part 16.4. The purpose of the particulars of claim is to set out the key elements of the claim that will be proved at trial so that the defendant(s) can respond and the issues in dispute for determination by the court can be identified. Boxes 4.3 and 4.4 list the elements that should typically be included in a claim.

The Queen's Bench Guide (CPR section 1B, paragraph 5.6) contains guidelines for the drafting of pleadings, referred to in the Guide as 'statements of case' (including particulars of claim, defence, reply, Part 20 claim):

Box 4.2: Model claim form

> In the High Court of Justice
> Queen's Bench Division
> Technology and Construction Court
> Claim No.
> Issue Date

Claimant: BAVARIAN POWER COMPANY LTD

Defendant(s): NEW DELHI ELECTRICITY LTD

Brief Details of Claim:

The claimant was engaged by the defendant under the MF/1 Model Form of Contract (as amended by the parties) to supply, install and commission a new 240 megawatt generator in the defendant's existing power station. The claimant claims an extension of the time for completion of the said works of 12 months and the sum of £1 million as sums due under the Contract and/or as damages.

Value: £1 million plus interest [or not less than £x]

Defendant's name and address

Amount claimed	
Court fee	
Solicitor's costs	
Total amount	

Does or will your claim include any issues under the Human Rights Act 1998? ☐ Yes ☐ No

Particulars of claim attached/to follow

Statement of truth

I believe that the facts stated in these particulars of claim are true.

Signed:

(1) a statement of case must be as brief and concise as possible
(2) a statement of case should be set out in separate consecutively numbered paragraphs and sub-paragraphs
(3) so far as possible each paragraph or sub-paragraph should contain no more than one allegation

Box 4.3: Elements of a typical engineering contract claim

- Parties – identify the parties to the contract.
- Contract – identify the material terms.
- Summary of the material facts – only those necessary to explain the claim.
- Claims made under the contract, e.g. certified sums due, variations, extensions of time, additional payment.
- Allegations of breach of contract – identify the terms breached.
- Damages claimed – identify the causal link between breaches and loss.
- Interest – state the basis of the claim for interest and, if for a specific sum, identify the rate and period applicable.

Box 4.4: Elements of a typical claim against an engineer

- Parties – identify the parties involved.
- Contract – identify the material terms.
- Duty of care – facts relied on to establish the special relationship and the standard of care required.
- Summary of the material facts – only those necessary to explain the claim.
- Particulars of the wrongful acts or omissions relied on.
- Allegations of breach of duty/breach of contract – identify the terms breached/failure to exercise reasonable skill and care.
- Damages claimed – identify the causal link between breaches/negligence and loss.
- Interest – state the basis of the claim for interest and, if for a specific sum, identify the rate and period applicable.

(4) the facts and matters alleged should be set out as far as reasonably possible in chronological order
(5) the statement of case should deal with the claim on a point by point basis, to allow a point by point response
(6) where a party is required to give reasons, the allegation should be stated first and then the reasons listed one by one in separate numbered sub-paragraphs
(7) a party wishing to advance a positive claim must identify that claim in the statement of case
(8) any matter which if not stated might take another party by surprise should be stated
(9) where they will assist, headings, abbreviations and definitions should be used and a glossary annexed; contentious headings, abbreviations, paraphrasing and definitions should not be used and every effort

should be made to ensure that they are in a form acceptable to the other parties

(10) particulars of primary allegations should be stated as particulars and not as primary allegations

(11) schedules or appendices should be used if this would be helpful, for example where lengthy particulars are necessary and any response should also be stated in a schedule or appendix

(12) any lengthy extracts from documents should be placed in a schedule.

All statements of case must be verified by a statement of truth (CPR Part 22.1), a statement that the party putting forward the document believes the facts stated in the document are true.

The defendant must acknowledge service of the claim form or file a defence within 14 days after service of the claim form or particulars of claim, whichever is later (CPR Part 10.3). Any challenge to the jurisdiction of the court (e.g. on the grounds that there is an arbitration agreement in the contract or the contract provides that the dispute should be tried in another jurisdiction) should be made by application following acknowledgement of service and before any further participation in the proceedings (CPR Part 11).

If a defendant wishes to defend the claim, a defence must be served (if not served instead of an acknowledgement of service – see above) within 28 days after service of the particulars of claim (CPR Part 15.4). In the TCC, where the factual and expert issues are complex, this period is often extended.

The requirements of the defence are set out in CPR Part 16.5. The defence must provide a comprehensive response to the particulars of claim and the defendant must state:

- which allegations in the particulars of claim are (i) admitted, (ii) denied, or (iii) allegations that the defendant is unable to admit or deny (e.g. where the allegation is inadequately particularised and further information or explanation is needed)
- if facts are disputed, the defendant's case as to the correct facts
- if allegations are denied, an explanation for such denial
- if quantum (value of the claim) is disputed, any principles on which the sums claimed are disputed (e.g. no loss arguments, wrong basis of calculation).

Where the defendant has a claim against the claimant and wishes to pursue it in the same proceedings (a counterclaim), such counterclaim can be made as a defence by way of set-off (if there is sufficient connection between the claim and the counterclaim) and/or as a separate counter-claim (CPR Part 16.6; CPR Part 20.4). A defendant is entitled as of right to serve a counterclaim with a defence, but if it is served later the permission of the court must be obtained (CPR Part 20.4).

The claimant is entitled but not compelled to serve a reply. If no reply is served, the matters set out in the defence are deemed to be in issue (CPR Part 16.7). A reply should be served in the following circumstances:

- where the claimant wishes to admit parts of the defence
- where the claimant wishes to respond to the defence by alleging facts that were not included in the particulars of claim.

Where the defendant has served a counterclaim, the claimant should serve a defence to counterclaim.

Any claim in proceedings other than a claim by a claimant against a defendant is known as a Part 20 Claim (CPR Part 20.2). Part 20 claims include:

- a counterclaim by a defendant
- a claim by a defendant against another party
- a claim by a defendant for contribution against another defendant.

A Part 20 claim is treated as if it were a claim for the purpose of preparing and serving pleadings (CPR Part 20.3).

Further pleadings
If the parties wish to file additional statements of case after the reply (e.g. a rejoinder to respond to a new issue raised in the reply), permission must be sought from the court and will only be given in exceptional circumstances where the matter cannot be dealt with conveniently by the amendment of other pleadings (CPR Part 15.9).

CPR Part 18 sets out the circumstances in which a party is entitled to further information in respect of the other party's case. The court may at any time order a party to:

- clarify any matter which is in dispute in the proceedings, or
- give additional information in relation to any such matter

whether or not the matter is contained in or referred to in a statement of case and in the absence of an application by any party (CPR Part 18.1).

A party may make an application under Part 18 (CPR Part 18.1; 18PD.1) provided that:

(1) a written request for such information has been made prior to the application – this can be set out in a letter rather than a formal document but should identify the title and number of the claim, set out each request in a separate numbered paragraph and identify the relevant document or part of the pleading to which it relates, or it can be in schedule form
(2) the party making the request has fixed a reasonable period of time for the response and no (or no adequate) response has been provided, and
(3) the further information requested is reasonably necessary and pro-portionate to enable the requesting party to understand the case it has to meet.

The response to a request for further information must be in writing, dated and signed by the party or the party's legal representative and verified by a statement of truth. If the request has been served in a schedule, the response should be inserted into an additional column in the schedule. Otherwise, the response should identify the title and number of the claim, repeat each request in a separate numbered paragraph and set out the response underneath.

Part 8 claims

The claim form in a Part 8 claim (where there is no substantial dispute of fact) must state (CPR Part 8.2):

(1) that it is a claim to which Part 8 applies, and
(2) the question which the claimant wants the court to decide or the remedy which the claimant is seeking and the legal basis for the claim to that remedy.

The claim form should not be lengthy. The question(s) for determination and the remedy sought should be identified concisely and the factual or legal basis for the claim should be in summary form. The claim form must be verified by a statement of truth (CPR Part 22.1). Any written evidence on which the claimant intends to rely should be filed and served with the claim form (CPR Part 8.5).

A defendant who wishes to respond to a Part 8 claim or to take an active part in the hearing must acknowledge service of the claim form within 14 days of service using form N210 (CPR Part 8.3, 8.4; CPR Practice Direction Part 8.3), stating:

(1) whether the defendant intends to dispute the claim
(2) if the defendant intends to dispute the claim, the grounds and any alternative remedy sought
(3) whether the defendant intends to contest the court's jurisdiction
(4) whether the defendant objects to the use of the Part 8 procedure, and if so on what grounds.

The acknowledgement of service must be verified by a statement of truth (CPR Part 22.1). Any written evidence on which the defendant intends to rely should be filed and served with the acknowledgement of service (CPR Part 8.5).

The claimant is entitled to file further written evidence in reply within 14 days of the service of the defendant's evidence (CPR Part 8.5).

Arbitration claims

Arbitration claims include any applications to the court under the Arbitration Act 1996 or otherwise concerned with arbitration (CPR Part 62), such as:

- challenge to an arbitration award on grounds of jurisdiction under section 67 of the 1996 Act (e.g. no contract, no valid appointment of arbitral panel, award outside ambit of dispute referred)
- challenge to an arbitration award on grounds of serious irregularity under section 68 (e.g. bias, misconduct of arbitration proceedings)
- appeal on a point of law under section 69
- application to enforce an arbitration award as if it were a judgment or order of the court under section 66

- a claim to determine whether there is a valid arbitration agreement or whether the arbitration tribunal is properly constituted.

An arbitration claim form (see Box 4.5) should be issued under Part 8 (see above) using form 8A and must (CPR Part 62.4, 62.18):

(1) include a concise statement of the remedy claimed and any questions on which the decision of the court is sought
(2) give details of the arbitration award challenged or to be enforced
(3) identify which parts of the award are challenged and set out the grounds on which the award is challenged
(4) show that any statutory requirements have been met (e.g. agreement between the parties that an appeal can be made)
(5) state under which section of the 1996 Act the claim is made
(6) identify any costs order sought against any defendant, and
(7) identify the persons on whom the arbitration claim will be served, or state that the claim is made without notice under section 44(3) of the 1996 Act (application to the court for an urgent order to preserve assets or evidence) setting out the grounds relied on, or state that the claim is made under sections 66 or 101 of the 1996 Act (enforcement).

The arbitration claim form must be served within 1 month from the date of issue unless the court orders otherwise (CPR Part 62.4(2)). The claimant may rely on the matters set out in the arbitration claim form as evidence (provided the statement of truth has been signed). In addition, the claimant may file witness statements in support of the arbitration claim, which must be served with the arbitration claim form.

A defendant who wishes to respond to the arbitration claim or to take active part in the hearing must acknowledge service of the arbitration claim form within 14 days of service using form 15A (this is not necessary if the arbitration application is made during the course of other court proceedings), stating:

(1) whether the defendant intends to dispute the arbitration claim and/or the claim for costs
(2) if the defendant intends to dispute the claim, the grounds and any alternative remedy sought
(3) whether the defendant intends to contest the court's jurisdiction.

An arbitrator who is sent an arbitration claim form may apply to the court to be made a defendant or to be permitted to make representations to the court (CPR Practice Direction Part 62, paragraph 4.1).

The acknowledgement of service must be verified by a statement of truth (CPR Part 22.1). Any written evidence on which the defendant intends to rely should be filed and served within 21 days from the date by which the defendant was required to serve the acknowledgement of service or, where no acknowledgement is required (e.g. where the application is made in ongoing proceedings), within 21 days after service of the arbitration claim form (CPR Practice Direction Part 62, paragraph 6.2).

Box 4.5: Model arbitration claim form

> In the High Court of Justice
> Queen's Bench Division
> Technology and Construction Court
> Claim No.
> Issue Date

In an arbitration claim between:

Claimant: BAVARIAN POWER COMPANY LTD
Defendant: NEW DELHI ELECTRICITY LTD

And in the matter of an arbitration between:

Claimant: BAVARIAN POWER COMPANY LTD
Respondent: NEW DELHI ELECTRICITY LTD

To the defendant:

This arbitration claim is made:

☐ without notice   ☐ on notice to the persons whose names are given above (or set out)

This arbitration claim will be heard by a judge sitting in public/private.

The hearing of this arbitration claim will take place in court [. . .] at [address] on [date] at [time] (or on a date to be fixed).

Grounds of claim and details of what is being claimed:

The claimant seeks orders pursuant to section 69(7) of the Arbitration Act 1996:

(a) allowing its appeal against the award of the Arbitrator Mr Black FCIArb made and published on the 30th day of November 2005;
(b) varying the award in whole or in part and/or remitting the award to the Arbitrator in whole or in part for reconsideration in the light of the court's determination of the issues determined by the Arbitrator.

The grounds of the claim are as follows:

1. The claimant was engaged by the defendant under the MF/1 Model Form of Contract (as amended by the parties) to supply, install and commission a new 240 megawatt generator in the defendant's existing power station.
2. The works were commenced on 1st April 2003 and carried out in accordance with the Contract. The Time for Completion within

the meaning of clause 32 was 12 months (i.e. by 1st April 2004) but delays occurred and the Taking Over Certificate was not issued in respect of the works until 1st April 2005.

3. On 15th July 2005 the claimant commenced arbitration proceedings against the defendant, claiming an extension of time of 12 months and additional payment in the sum of £1 million caused by numerous and late variations instructed by the defendant.

4. In the award the Arbitrator found in favour of the claimant on time but awarded £50,000 only in respect of the additional costs claimed.

5. The Arbitrator erred in law in holding that the Engineer's valuation of variations under clause 27 of the Contract was final and binding.

6. The Arbitrator should have made an independent assessment of the sums due to the claimant in respect of the variations claimed and should have valued the additional costs at £1 million as claimed.

The claimant seeks an order for costs against New Delhi Electricity Ltd.

Statement of truth
I believe that the facts stated in this arbitration claim form are true.

Signed:

The claimant is entitled to file further written evidence in reply within 7 days of the service of the defendant's evidence (CPR Practice Direction Part 62, paragraph 6.3).

Unless otherwise ordered by the court, automatic directions are applicable, as set out in CPR Practice Direction Part 62, paragraph 6:

(1) The claimant must prepare an agreed bundle of all documents to be used at the hearing, paginated and indexed.

(2) The bundle must be filed at court not later than 5 days before the hearing date together with an estimate of the length of the hearing.

(3) Not later than 2 days before the hearing the claimant must file with the court and serve on other parties:
   (a) chronology
   (b) list of persons involved, and
   (c) skeleton argument identifying *concisely* the issues, the grounds relied on, any submissions of fact and the submissions of law.

(4) Not later than the day before the hearing the defendant must file with the court and serve on the other parties a skeleton argument as above.

In arbitration claims or applications of any substance, the practice in the TCC is for bundles and skeletons to be filed earlier than set out in the practice direction. If in doubt, the parties should seek directions from the court as to an appropriate timetable.

Adjudication enforcement proceedings

Section 108 of the Housing Grants, Construction and Regeneration Act 1996 introduced a mandatory right for a party to a construction contract to refer a dispute arising under the contract at any time for determination by adjudication.

Where a party wishes to enforce an adjudication award for a sum of money, a claim form should be issued under CPR Part 7. If there is no substantial issue of fact and declaratory relief only is sought, a claim form should be issued under CPR Part 8.

The TCC has a special procedure for dealing with adjudication enforcement proceedings (TCC Guide, paragraph 9.2: CPR 2C-91).

The claim form should:

(1) identify the construction contract (including the parties, date and documents in which the contract was contained or evidenced)
(2) state the jurisdiction of the adjudicator and the procedural rules under which the adjudication was conducted
(3) set out a summary of the adjudicator's decision, and
(4) state the relief sought and the grounds for seeking that relief.

The following documents should be served with the claim form:

(1) Application notice seeking summary judgment under CPR Part 24 (see the section 'Summary judgment').
(2) Application for abridgement of time for acknowledgement of service by the defendant, time for service of any evidence by the defendant and an early return date for the hearing of the application, and
(3) Witness statements setting out the evidence relied on in support of the applications, including a copy of the adjudication decision.

The papers should be marked: 'paper without notice adjudication enforcement claim and application for the urgent attention of a TCC judge' and an estimate given for the hearing. The claim will be assigned to a TCC judge, who will give speedy directions (usually within 3 days) for the service of evidence, bundles, skeletons and the date for the hearing (usually within 28 days of the directions).

Applications for declaratory relief (e.g. disputed jurisdiction of the adjudicator, dispute as to whether there was a valid construction contract) will be assigned to a TCC judge and a case management conference fixed promptly (usually within 2 days) so that directions can be given for the dispute to be resolved without causing any significant delay to the adjudication process (TCC Guide, paragraph 9.4: CPR 2C-93).

Case management

As mentioned above, the overriding objective of the CPR is to determine claims justly, ensuring that the parties are on an equal footing, saving expense, dealing with the case in a way that is proportionate to the size and complexity of the case and the court's resources and ensuring that the disputes are dealt with expeditiously and fairly (CPR Part 1.1). In the TCC, it is expected that the parties will cooperate so as to assist in achieving that objective.

The first case management conference (CMC) will be fixed by the court within 14 days of the filing of an acknowledgement of service, a defence or an order transferring the claim to the TCC (CPR Practice Direction Part 60, paragraph 8.1). The court will consider any proposals for CMCs and any other applications in the claim to be dealt with by telephone, video link or on paper in appropriate cases (CPR Practice Direction Part 60, paragraph 4).

Each party is required to prepare certain documents for the first CMC (see Boxes 4.6–4.8) unless they are agreed. The documents must be filed at

---

Box 4.6: Checklist of documents for first CMC

- Case management information sheet (Box 4.7).
- List of proposed directions (Box 4.8).
- Pre-Action Protocol material.
- Any additional applications (e.g. to join additional parties).

Box 4.7: Matters to be dealt with in the CMC information sheet

- Settlement – is a stay of the proceedings required so that the parties can attempt to settle?
- Location of trial – reasons should be given for any preference expressed.
- Pre-Action Protocols – confirmation that the parties have complied or explanation if not.
- Case management information – size of claim and any counterclaim.
- Applications – identify any other applications, e.g. summary judgment.
- Witnesses – preliminary identification of the relevant factual witnesses and issues addressed.
- Experts – identify the experts and field of expertise. The parties should consider whether a single joint expert would be appropriate (e.g. for quantum).
- Disclosure – state any special orders sought (e.g. issues of confidentiality, proposal for limited disclosure).
- Transfer – consider whether the claim should be dealt with in another division or in a county court.
- Estimate of trial length and availability of witnesses.
- Proposed directions (see below) – these should be attached to the sheet and agreed where possible.
- Costs – estimate of costs to date and overall costs.

Box 4.8: Items to be included in the list of proposed directions

- Trial date and estimated length of trial.
- Consideration whether any stay for alternative dispute resolution should be ordered.
- Directions for preliminary issues or sub-trials – the parties should consider whether there are key issues that could usefully be determined in advance of the main trial (section 8 of the TCC Guide).
- Consolidation with any other related claims and consideration of any additional Part 20 claims.
- Further statements of case – defence and counterclaim, reply and defence to counterclaim.
- Permission to make amendments.
- Scott Schedule (a table setting out each defect, variation or financial claim together with the basis for each claim) – directions for contents of each column and time for service and response by the parties.
- Disclosure of documents – provision for paper and electronic disclosure.
- Date for service of factual witness statements.
- Permission for expert evidence – the issues or disciplines should be identified.
- Directions for calculations/tests by experts, without prejudice meetings, joint statements and expert reports.
- Directions for any single joint expert.
- Direction for provision of documents electronically to the court.
- Date for further CMC.
- Date for pre-trial review.
- Procedural rules for any changes to the timetable (agreed changes can often be dealt with on paper without the need for a hearing).
- Liberty to restore (the parties do not need to issue fresh applications to raise additional CMC issues, although separate applications are required for other interlocutory matters).
- Costs in the case.

court and served on all parties at least 2 days before the CMC (in larger cases, this should be done much earlier to enable the parties to agree as much as possible) (CPR Practice Direction Part 60, paragraph 8.3).

Alternative dispute resolution

CPR Part 1.4 requires the court to further the overriding objective by actively managing cases, and active case management includes encouraging the parties to use an alternative dispute resolution (ADR) procedure if the court considers that appropriate. ADR is defined, rather unhelpfully, as a 'collective description of methods of resolving

---

Box 4.9: Draft ADR order

1. By [   ] the parties shall exchange lists of three neutral individuals who have indicated their availability to conduct a mediation/ENE in this case prior to [   ].
2. By [   ] the parties shall agree an individual from the exchanged lists to conduct the mediation/ENE by [   ]. If the parties are unable to agree on the neutral individual, they will apply to the Court in writing by [   ] and the Court will choose one of the listed individuals to conduct the mediation/ENE.
3. There will be a stay of the proceedings until [   ] to allow the mediation/ENE to take place. On or before that date, the Court shall be informed as to whether or not the case has been finally settled. If it has not been finally settled, the parties will:
   (a) comply with all outstanding directions made by the Court;
   (b) attend for a review CMC on [   ].

---

disputes otherwise than through the normal trial process'. In the TCC Guide, ADR is taken to mean any process through which the parties attempt to resolve their dispute which is voluntary, and in most cases ADR takes the form of mediation conducted by a neutral mediator (see Chapter 7). Alternative forms of ADR include formal inter-party negotiations or (occasionally) early neutral evaluation (see Chapter 9) (TCC Guide, paragraph 7.1.1).

At any stage after the first CMC (see the CMC information sheet, referred to above) prior to the commencement of trial, the court will, either on its own initiative or if requested to do so by one or both of the parties, consider whether to facilitate ADR, often by granting a short stay in the proceedings. It should be noted that the court's role is to encourage ADR, not to compel it (*Halsey* v. *Milton Keynes General NHS Trust* [2004] EWCA Civ 576; [2004] 1WLR 3002 (CA)). Alternatively, the court may simply encourage the parties to seek ADR and allow for it to occur within the timetable for the resolution of the proceedings set down by the court without a formal stay of the proceedings.

If the court does consider it appropriate, an ADR order may be made. A draft ADR order appears in Appendix E to the TCC Guide and is reproduced above (Box 4.9).

Summary judgment

A party to proceedings should consider whether there are any short cuts that can be taken to obtain relief or resolution prior to a full trial, such as summary judgment.

The court may give summary judgment against a party (determine the claim or an issue without a full trial) if (CPR Part 24.2):

(1) it considers that the claimant has no real prospect of succeeding on the claim or issue, or that the defendant has no real prospect of successfully defending the claim or issue, and

(2) there is no other compelling reason why the case or issue should be disposed of at trial.

An applicant may not apply for summary judgment until the defendant to the application has filed an acknowledgement of service or defence (save where the court orders otherwise). When an application for summary judgment has been issued prior to the service of the defence, the defendant is not required to serve a defence until after the application (CPR Part 24.4).

In the TCC, the applicant should obtain a suitable date and time from the court before issuing the application and should then serve the application notice (see Box 4.10) and evidence in support sufficiently in advance of the fixed date so as to enable the respondent to serve evidence in response and, generally, no less than 10 working days before the hearing date (TCC Guide, paragraph 6.2.4). In complex cases, directions should be sought from the court.

CPR Part 24.5 provides that if a respondent wishes to rely on written evidence the witness evidence must be filed with the court and served on other parties at least 7 days prior to the hearing. Any evidence in reply must be served by the applicant at least 3 days before the hearing. All witness statements should be verified by a statement of truth.

A paginated bundle should be provided to the court not less than 2 working days before the hearing and skeleton arguments should be served by each party.

Box 4.10: Formalities for an application notice

(1) The application notice must state that it is an application for summary judgment made under CPR Part 24.
(2) The application notice must state what order is sought – it must identify precisely the claim(s) or issue(s) in respect of which summary judgment is sought.
(3) The application notice or any evidence served with it must:

- identify concisely any point of law or provision in a document on which the applicant relies, and/or
- state that it is made because the applicant believes that on the evidence the respondent has no real prospect of succeeding on the claim or issue or of successfully defending the claim or issue to which the application relates, and in any event
- state that the applicant knows of no other reason why the disposal of the claim or issue should await trial.

(4) The evidence relied on in support of the application must be contained in or identified in the application notice and verified by a statement of truth.
(5) The application notice should draw the attention of the respondent to Rule 24.5.1 (see below).

In order to defend a Part 24 application, it is sufficient to show a real prospect or chance of success. It should be more than a fanciful prospect, but the court should not embark on a mini trial if the case is reasonably arguable (*Swain* v. *Hillman* [2001] 1 All ER 91 (CA); *Three Rivers District Council* v. *Bank of England (No. 3)* [2001] 2 All ER 513 (HL)).

On hearing a Part 24 application, the court can grant summary judgment of a claim, strike out or dismiss a claim, make a conditional order (e.g. a claim can be defended on condition that money is paid into court), give directions for the trial of the claim or make an order as to costs.

Interim payment

The court can make an order for an interim payment to be made in respect of a claim (CPR Part 25.7) if:

(1) the defendant has admitted liability to pay damages or some other sum of money to the claimant, or
(2) the claimant has obtained judgment against the defendant on liability with damages to be assessed, or
(3) the court is satisfied that at trial the claimant would obtain judgment for a substantial amount of money on the claim against the defendant.

The claimant may not make an application for interim payment until the time for filing an acknowledgement of service has expired (CPR Part 25.6). The application notice must be served at least 14 days before the hearing of the application and must be supported by evidence. If a respondent wishes to rely on written evidence the witness evidence must be filed with the court and served on other parties at least 7 days prior to the hearing. Any evidence in reply must be served by the applicant at least 3 days before the hearing. All witness statements should be verified by a statement of truth.

The court has a wide discretion as to whether to make any order (*Schott Kem Ltd* v. *Bentley* [1991] 1 QB 61 (CA)). Very often, any sum awarded will be assessed on a rough and ready basis. The court must not order an interim payment of more than a reasonable proportion of the likely amount of the final judgment and must take into account alleged contributory negligence and any relevant set off or counterclaim (CPR Part 25.6).

Interim injunction

An injunction is a court order prohibiting a person from doing something or requiring a person to do something. An injunction may be granted by the court at the end of a trial where the claimant has established a right in law and an infringement of that right by the defendant, such as carrying out engineering works on the land of another without permission. However, the court has a discretion to grant an interim injunction pending trial (CPR Part 25.1).

The application for an injunction should be made by an application notice setting out the order sought by the applicant and brief grounds relied on and should be filed with the court and served on the respondent together with a draft order and any witness statement in support, setting out all material facts, verified by a statement of truth (CPR 25PD.2). In urgent cases the application may be made without notice to the respondent, and in very urgent cases the application may be made out of court hours and/or by telephone (CPR 25PD.4).

On hearing the application, the court will not determine the issue on a final basis but will carry out a balancing exercise (*American Cyanamid* v. *Ethicon* [1975] AC 396 (HL)) by reference to the following questions (known as the '*Cyanamid* guidelines'):

(1) Does the applicant have a good arguable claim?
(2) Is there a serious issue to be tried?
(3) Would damages be an adequate remedy for the applicant (instead of an injunction)?
(4) Would damages be an adequate remedy for the respondent (if the injunction were found to be wrongly granted at trial)?
(5) Does the balance of convenience favour granting or refusing the injunction?

Generally, the applicant is required to give an undertaking to pay damages if the injunction proves to be wrongly granted at trial, but this is not a strict pre-condition for an interim injunction if there are special circumstances.

The *Cyanamid* guidelines are not relevant to applications for mandatory injunctions, i.e. where the court orders the respondent to do something (*Zockoll Group Ltd* v. *Mercury Communications Ltd* [1998] FSR 354 (CA)). In such cases the court will adopt the course that is likely to involve the least risk of injustice if it turns out be wrong, and generally it is necessary for the applicant to show that it has a strong and clear case in order to obtain a mandatory injunction (*Nottingham Building Society* v. *Eurodynamics Systems* [1993] FSR 468).

The court may grant a 'freezing injunction' restraining a party from removing assets from the jurisdiction (e.g. transferring funds abroad) or from dealing with assets within the jurisdiction (e.g. selling a development and spending the funds released) where there is a real risk that a party might dissipate its assets so as to avoid a judgment (*Mareva Compania Naviera SA* v. *International Bulkcarriers SA* [1975] 2 Ll.Rep.509 (CA)). An application for a freezing injunction must be supported by affidavit evidence (a written and sworn statement) (CPR Practice Directions Part 25.3).

Disclosure

Disclosure is the process whereby the parties disclose to each other documents relating to the issues in the claim, including documents that assist the other party, so as to enable a fair trial of the matter.

Standard disclosure rules require disclosure only of documents which are or were in a party's possession (including a right to possession or to inspect or take copies) (CPR Part 31.6 and 31.8):

(1) on which the party relies, and

(2) which (a) adversely affect the party's own case or (b) adversely affect another party's case or (c) support another party's case, and

(3) which the party is required to disclose by a relevant practice direction form.

The duty is an ongoing one.

In the TCC, parties are invited to consider whether there should be any limit on the disclosure ordered (e.g. to specific categories), or to dispense with formal disclosure, so as to reduce the volume of documents disclosed and the costs.

Disclosure is generally by list (CPR Part 31.10). The list should:

(1) identify the documents in a convenient order and manner and as concisely as possible

(2) identify any documents that are not available for inspection (e.g. privilege claimed)

(3) identify any documents that are no longer in the party's control, stating what has happened to them, and

(4) include a disclosure statement setting out the extent of the search made to locate the disclosable documents, certifying that the party understands the duty to disclose documents and to the best of his knowledge he has complied with that duty.

The parties should consider, and attempt to agree, any special orders required, e.g. for translation of foreign documents, disclosure in tranches or disclosure of electronic statements including database systems (TCC Guide, paragraph 11.2).

A party that considers that inadequate disclosure has been given may make an application for specific disclosure, requiring another party to disclose specific documents or categories or to carry out a search for such documents (CPR Part 31.12). The application should be made by issuing an application notice, setting out the order sought and be supported by evidence explaining the existence or probable existence of the documents sought and why disclosure was necessary for a fair trial (CPR Practice Direction Part 31.5). In considering the application, the court will take into account the overriding objective in CPR Part 1 but will only make an order if it is proportionate in all the circumstances.

Witness statements

Evidence at a trial should be given generally by oral evidence, i.e. the witnesses of fact should present themselves for examination by the other parties and the court so as to test their direct evidence. The purpose of witness statements (see Box 4.11) is to provide advance warning to the other parties of the evidence to be given so that facts can be agreed where possible and preparation carried out for an efficient hearing.

Generally, at trial the witness statement will stand as evidence-in-chief. Where recollection or credibility are in issue, the court may permit oral evidence-in-chief so as to obtain the witness's account on specific issues.

If a witness is unwilling or unable to provide a witness statement, the party seeking to rely on that witness's evidence at trial should

> **Box 4.11:** Contents of witness statements
>
> • A witness statement should be signed by the witness and verified by a statement of truth.
> • Documents should not be appended to the statement and the statement should not contain lengthy extracts from documents.
> • The statement should be in the witness's own words as far as possible.
> • The witness should make clear what evidence is based on the witness's own knowledge and what evidence is hearsay or a matter of belief.
> • A witness statement should be concise and not argumentative.
>
> (TCC Guide, paragraph 12.1)

prepare and serve a witness summary instead of the statement (CPR Part 32.9).

If a party intends to rely on 'hearsay evidence', i.e. evidence not given directly by a witness at trial or documentary records not made by a witness giving evidence, notice should be given of such intention stating the reason why direct evidence will not be called (CPR Part 33.2).

Although generally witnesses are expected to attend the trial when required by the court, in appropriate circumstances their evidence can be given by video link.

Expert reports

Expert evidence is evidence on technical or scientific matters given by a person with relevant expertise, including opinion evidence. The overriding duty of an expert is to help the court on matters within the expert's area of expertise (CPR Part 35.3). Expert evidence should be independent, regardless of the implications for the party instructing the expert, and should take account of all material facts, including those which might cast doubt on the expert's opinion.

Generally, the TCC will direct experts of like disciplines to meet to discuss the issues on a without prejudice basis. It is sensible for the parties or the experts to draw up a list of expert issues and an agenda for each meeting to ensure efficient use of time. The purpose of the meetings is to clarify the issues, exchange information and views, narrow the differences and reach agreement where possible. Any matters discussed or views expressed in the meetings must not be disclosed to the court.

Following the experts' meetings, usually the court will order the experts to produce a joint statement under CPR Part 35.12, in which the experts identify the issues agreed and those not agreed, with a short summary of the reasons for any disagreement (see Box 4.12). The legal advisors should not attend the meetings and should not be involved in negotiating or drafting the joint statement (TCC Guide, paragraph 13.6).

Box 4.12: Form and content of expert reports

- An expert report should be addressed to the court.
- The expert's qualifications should be set out (usually in an appendix).
- The report should set out the substance of all facts and instructions received that are material to the opinion expressed and identify any facts that are within the expert's own knowledge.
- The report should identify all relevant documents relied on, including published technical literature.
- The reports should state who carried out any tests or calculations relied on and explain the expert's role (e.g. supervisory).
- Where there is a range of opinion on the issues, the report should summarise that range of opinion and give reasons for the expert's own opinion.
- The report should set out a summary of the conclusions reached.
- The report should state clearly when any issue falls outside the expert's own expertise or for any other reason the expert is unable to reach a concluded view.
- The report should contain a statement that the expert understands the duty to the court and has complied with and will continue to comply with that duty.
- The expert's report must be verified by a statement of truth.
- If, after producing the report, the expert changes an opinion, the expert should notify the court and all parties as soon as possible.

(CPR Practice Direction Part 35)

Pre-trial review

The purpose of the pre-trial review (PTR) is to check that the parties are ready for trial and to determine the arrangements for the trial.

The parties should complete the PTR questionnaire and return it to the court in good time before the PTR (TCC Guide, paragraph 14), providing the following information:

(1) Compliance with previous directions and explanation for any non-compliance.
(2) Details of experts to be called – their meetings, joint statement and reports.
(3) Details of factual witnesses, availability and any special needs.
(4) Details of legal representation at the trial.
(5) Estimate of trial length.
(6) Estimated number of pages of evidence to be included in the trial bundles.

(7) Case summary.
(8) List of issues, agreed if possible.
(9) Proposals, agreed if possible, for directions to be given at the PTR.

At the PTR, the court will give directions for bundles, written and oral openings, timetable for evidence, transcripts and any other matters required to ensure a fair and efficient trial (TCC Guide, paragraphs 14, 15).

Trial

Generally, written opening submissions are required from each party in advance of the hearing. They do not have to be lengthy but should provide an overview of the case and an outline of the party's case in relation to each issue. The claimant should produce a chronology and *dramatis personae*. In large cases, a reading list is often ordered.

There is no fixed rule but often in TCC cases all factual evidence is heard first, followed by the expert witnesses for each discipline.

Witness evidence in court is usually taken on oath or affirmation. The witness is identified and confirms his or her witness statement(s). Sometimes a few introductory questions-in-chief are permitted and then the witness is tendered for cross-examination. When all other parties have had an opportunity to cross-examine, the party calling the witness is permitted to re-examine on any issues raised in cross-examination.

Permission of the court must be sought to introduce new witnesses, new documentary evidence or new expert material. The court will consider whether in all the circumstances the evidence should be admitted so as to ensure a fair hearing without prejudicing the other parties. Late introduction of evidence is to be avoided because it carries with it the risk of an adjournment and/or cost penalties.

Closing submissions may be made orally at the close of evidence or there may be a short adjournment of the trial to enable the parties to produce written submissions, possibly with a further short hearing.

In all but the simplest of trials in the TCC, judgment is reserved and produced in writing.

Costs

Engineering claims can be expensive to fight. A claimant should check that the defendant has funds to pay any judgment as there is little to be gained by victory against an impecunious party. The court has power to make costs cap orders (TCC Guide, paragraph 16.3) but they are rarely appropriate in complex engineering claims.

Interlocutory hearings that last one day or less will usually be the subject of a summary assessment of costs (CPR Part 44.7). The parties must ensure that statements of costs are filed with the court and served on the other parties at least 24 hours before the hearing (TCC Guide, paragraph 16.2.1). For longer or more complex applications and trials, costs are subject to a detailed assessment if not agreed.

A defendant (including a defendant to a counterclaim) has the opportunity to seek security for costs in respect of the claim against it by provision of a guarantee, bond or payment into court (CPR Part 25.12). The application should be made by application notice supported by written evidence. The court has a discretion to make an order for security (see Box 4.13) if it is satisfied that:

Box 4.13: Factors taken into account by the court when determining costs

- Whether the claim is bona fide or a sham (does it have any apparent merit?).
- Whether there is any admission by the defendant, any open offer or payment into court.
- Whether the application is being made oppressively, i.e. to stop the defence.
- Whether any want of means on the part of the defendant has been caused by the claimant, e.g. failure to pay sums due.
- Whether the application is made at a late stage in the proceedings.

(*Sir Lindsay Parkinson* v. *Triplan Ltd* [1973] QB 609 (CA))

---

(1) having regard to all the circumstances of the case it is just to make an order, and
(2) one of the following conditions applies (CPR Part 25.13):

- the claimant is resident out of the jurisdiction
- the claimant is a company or other body and there is reason to believe that it will be unable to pay the defendant's costs if ordered to do so (see also section 726(1) of the Companies Act 1985)
- the claimant has failed to give an address, given a false address or changed address with a view to avoiding payment
- the claimant is a nominal claimant and there is reason to believe them to be unable to pay the defendant's costs if ordered to do so
- the claimant has taken steps in relation to assets that would make it difficult to enforce an order for costs.

A party can protect itself against a costs order by making a Part 36 offer and/or payment into court (CPR Part 36):

- A Part 36 offer must be in writing.
- A Part 36 offer may relate to the whole claim or part or any specific issue.
- A Part 36 offer must state:

  (1) whether it relates to the whole claim or any part, and if so which part
  (2) whether it takes into account any counterclaim, and
  (3) whether it is inclusive of interest.

- A Part 36 offer made not less than 21 days before the start of the trial must:

(1) be expressed to remain open for acceptance for 21 days from the date of the offer, and
(2) provide that after the 21-day period the offer can be accepted only if the parties agree liability for costs or with permission of the court.

- A Part 36 offer made less than 21 days before the start of the trial must state that it can be accepted only if the parties agree liability for costs or with permission of the court.
- The court must not be informed of the offer until after the hearing.

If the offer is accepted, the claim is automatically stayed and the claimant is entitled to its costs (CPR Parts 36.13, 14, 15). If the offer is not accepted (and not withdrawn), when liability and quantum have been determined at the hearing:

- if the claimant fails to better the defendant's offer or payment, the general rule is that the claimant will have to pay the defendant's costs from the date when the offer or payment could have been accepted (CPR Part 36.20).
- If the claimant betters its own claimant's offer (i.e. settles for a smaller sum than the full claim), the general rule is that the defendant will have to pay interest on the award at a rate not exceeding 10% above base rate, costs on an indemnity basis and interest on those costs at a rate not exceeding 10% above base rate (CPR Part 36.21).

The court has complete discretion as to orders for costs (CPR Part 44.3). Subject to the above, the general rule is that costs follow the event, i.e. the overall winner is awarded costs. However, the CPR require the courts to be more ready to make separate orders which reflect the outcome of different issues (*Phonographic Performance Ltd* v. *AEI Rediffusion Music Ltd* [1999] 2 All ER 299; *Johnsey Estates Ltd* v. *Secretary of State for the Department Environment, Transport and the Regions* [2001] EWCA 535). Where a party has exaggerated a claim or pursued unreasonable issues, it may be appropriate to make a percentage reduction in the recoverable costs (*English* v. *Emery Reimbold & Strick Ltd* [2002] 1 WLR 2409 (CA)).

Generally, costs are ordered to be paid on the standard basis (costs have to be reasonably incurred and proportionate) although there is power to order costs on the indemnity basis (costs have to be reasonably incurred) if the court wishes to express disapproval of the conduct of the trial (CPR Part 44.4; *McPhilemy* v. *Times Newspapers Ltd (No. 2)* [2004] 4 All ER 861 (CA)).

It may be argued that there should be a departure from the general rule on costs because one or more parties unreasonably refused to take part in ADR. As a matter of principle, the burden is on the unsuccessful party to show why there should be such a departure from the general rule, and the Court of Appeal has in *Halsey* v. *Milton Keynes General NHS Trust* [2004] EWCA Civ 576, [2004] 1 WLR 3002 (CA) identified six factors that may be relevant to any such consideration:

- the nature of the dispute
- the merits of the case

- the extent to which other settlement methods have been attempted
- whether the costs of the ADR would be disproportionate
- whether any delay in setting up and attending the ADR would have been prejudicial
- whether the ADR had a reasonable prospect of success.

As noted above, the court's role is to encourage, not to compel, ADR, but where the court has made an ADR order it will expect each party to cooperate fully with any ADR which takes place, and adverse cost consequences may flow if a party does not.

Appeals

If a party is dissatisfied with an order or judgment of the court, it can seek a review of the decision by the Court of Appeal.

Permission is required for an appeal from most TCC judgments or orders (CPR Part 52.3; *Tanfern Ltd* v. *Cameron-MacDonald* [2000] 1 WLR 1311 (CA)). Permission should first be requested from the TCC (when the judgment or order is made) and, if refused, from the Court of Appeal (applications are usually determined on paper although an oral hearing will be allowed in very complex cases). Permission to appeal will only be given where:

(1) the court considers that the appeal would have a real prospect of success (e.g. an obvious mistake by the judge or conflicting authorities), or

(2) there is some other compelling reason why the appeal should be heard (e.g. matter of public importance).

The procedure within the Court of Appeal is beyond the scope of this book.

5. Arbitration

Paul Buckingham

What is arbitration?

Although arbitration has been employed for resolving disputes in England for centuries, there is a noticeable absence of an accepted definition that is sufficiently wide to encompass the many different aspects of arbitration practice. However, at its most fundamental, arbitration is a private form of final and binding dispute resolution by a third party, based upon the agreement of the parties and according to the applicable law of the contract. The key features which distinguish arbitration from other forms of dispute resolution are:

- It is private – whereas the court system in England is provided by the state and open to the public, arbitration is a private method of resolving disputes that is funded by the parties themselves.
- It is final and binding – other methods of dispute resolution, such as mediation, conciliation and adjudication, are generally neither final nor binding unless the parties agree otherwise or decide not to continue further with a dispute. Except for very limited circumstances, arbitration is final and binding, and an arbitration award will generally be enforced by the courts if one party fails to comply. Arbitration is regulated under the Arbitration Act 1996, which sets out a detailed framework for the regulation and enforcement of arbitration in England, Wales and Northern Ireland.
- A decision is made by a third party – a mediator, for example, attempts to bring the parties together to reach a mutually agreeable settlement of the issues in dispute, and does not issue a decision on the dispute itself. An arbitrator is like a judge and, having considered all the evidence, will reach a decision.
- It is based upon the agreement of the parties – arbitration is consensual, therefore the parties have to agree to resolve disputes through arbitration rather than rely upon the court, which would otherwise be the default position.
- The decision is according to applicable law of the contract.

A common misconception is that choosing to have disputes resolved through arbitration in London will mean that the underlying disputes will be determined according to English law. This is not necessarily the case. The tribunal will apply the governing law stated in the contract.

Note that care must be taken to draw a distinction between expert determination and arbitration: whilst expert determination is also a final and binding form of dispute resolution by a third party, it is not regulated and enforced by statute (Arbitration Act 1996). It is therefore more suited to the resolution of discrete issues, such as a particular technical or valuation dispute, where it can provide a speedy and cost effective resolution (see Chapter 8).

Advantages of arbitration

Arbitration has a number of advantages over litigation:

- Privacy and confidentiality – arbitration allows the parties to keep their disputes private and confidential. (In this context, privacy means that the general public has no right to attend a hearing before the tribunal. Confidentiality refers to restrictions on the use of documents disclosed in an arbitration by the parties.) This is of course in contrast to the very public nature of litigation before the courts. However, confidentiality can be lost if one of the parties attempts to appeal an award before the court.
- Enforceability – arbitration awards in England are enforceable by the courts under the Arbitration Act 1996 in very much the same way as a judgment of the court. Internationally, arbitration awards are readily enforceable in many countries under the 1958 New York Convention on the Recognition and Enforcement of Foreign Arbital Awards. This convention has been ratified or acceded to by some two-thirds of the countries recognised by the United Nations, which means that an arbitration award in one convention state is readily enforceable in another convention state. This is important in the context of international disputes (see Chapter 10), and is one of the primary reasons why arbitration is the preferred method of dispute resolution for international construction and engineering projects.
- Flexibility and formality – the fact that the parties have agreed to resolve disputes privately allows them more control over the procedure, including the manner in which evidence is provided and witnesses examined. There are no restrictions on who can represent a party (as opposed to the restrictions in the English Courts), and the parties often agree upon the timing and venue for the arbitration rather than having those factors determined by the court.
- Technical expertise – the parties are free to decide and agree upon the arbitrator (or arbitrators) to decide their dispute. Accordingly, for a very technical dispute the parties can appoint an arbitrator with technical expertise in that particular field, or if the matter raises specific legal issues, they may appoint a legal practitioner eminent in that area of the law. In both cases arbitration allows the parties to choose whom they would prefer to determine the dispute between them.
- Speed and cost – for many small construction disputes arbitration is significantly quicker and cheaper than litigation. However, the same cannot be said for complex disputes, where the magnitude of documentary and witness evidence is likely to determine both the cost and duration of the proceedings. Having said that, arbitration is, of course, flexible and allows the parties to implement appropriate

measures to maintain the efficiency of the proceedings by, for example, limiting the number of documents disclosed or restricting the length of hearing time.

• Neutrality – arbitration is a politically neutral means of dispute resolution. Internationally, parties are often reluctant to rely upon the local courts for resolving disputes if one of the parties is a state entity, and therefore arbitration at a neutral venue is the general compromise.

• Finality – arbitration is a final form of dispute resolution, with only very limited grounds for challenge. These generally relate to improper procedure or conduct by the tribunal, such as, for example, bias on the part of one of the arbitrators. Under the Arbitration Act 1996, there is a further right of appeal on points of law, but that right is strictly limited and means that parties are, in reality, rarely able to challenge an arbitration award.

Disadvantages of arbitration

There are, however, a number of disadvantages to arbitration:

• Pre-emptive remedies – as the parties have agreed that disputes are to be determined by arbitration, a tribunal has to be appointed and established before either party can seek and obtain a remedy. This can give rise to problems in relation to urgent applications, such as injunctions. In addition, even if the tribunal has the power to grant pre-emptive remedies, it does not have jurisdiction to commit a party for contempt in the event of non-compliance, with the result that pre-emptive orders of the tribunal are coercive rather than mandatory. Nevertheless, the courts have the powers to grant interim or interlocutory relief in support of an arbitration, which can often provide the parties with the necessary remedy.

• Joinder of parties – arbitration is private and consensual in nature, so only those parties which have agreed to arbitrate can be a party to the arbitration itself. Therefore, it is often not possible to join a third party (such as a subcontractor) into an existing arbitration (between employer and main contractor) unless all parties consent. Once a dispute has arisen it can be very difficult, if not impossible, for parties to agree upon anything. If the intention is to have multi-party arbitrations covering all parties to a large project, that can only be achieved through careful drafting of the contractual documentation, not after disputes have arisen.

• Parallel proceedings – the courts are reluctant to allow litigation where a similar dispute is already pending before another court (whether in the same country or elsewhere). However, because arbitration arises from the arbitration agreement in a specific contract, parties run the risk of multiple arbitrations if there is a series of linked but different contracts between the same parties in respect of the same project. In particular, the recent growth in the number of bilateral investment treaty arbitrations means that a party could be faced with the prospect of defending a number of arbitrations arising out of the same facts but different contractual relationships, resulting in the possibility of inconsistent findings.

The arbitration clause

The arbitration clause within a contract is the basis of the agreement of the parties to refer disputes to arbitration, and it is important that the clause is properly drafted to ensure that it operates in the manner in which the parties intended. One of the first steps in establishing how an arbitration is to proceed is to decide whether the arbitration should be carried out under a set of institutional rules, or by an 'ad hoc' arrangement between the parties.

Institutional arbitration

There are many established institutions whose arbitration rules have developed over a considerable period of time and address all the issues likely to be encountered in the conduct of an arbitration. Among the more prominent institutions are:

- the International Court of Arbitration (ICC), based in Paris
- the London Court of International Arbitration (LCIA), based in London
- the Stockholm Chamber of Commerce (SCC)
- the American Arbitration Association (AAA)
- the International Centre for Settlement of Investment Disputes (ICSID).

Each of these institutions has its own set of rules, and the great advantage of using these rules is that the administration of the arbitration is carried out by that institution. Therefore, the scope for disputes as to the procedure are reduced, ensuring that a tribunal is appointed relatively quickly and efficiently. (These rules are also of international application and so are addressed in further detail in Chapter 10.) However, the fact that the institution discharges the administration means that this form of arbitration is generally more expensive.

Ad hoc arbitration

Rather than have an institutionally supervised arbitration, the parties can agree upon a set of procedural rules and manage the arbitration themselves.

The most commonly adopted set of procedural rules are those of the United Nations Commission on International Trade Law (UNCITRAL) of 1976. The rules were specifically designed for use across the world in ad hoc arbitrations and provide a perfectly adequate procedure to allow an arbitration to progress successfully. However, it is important to note that there is no default appointing authority, and therefore any party considering using these rules should nominate an appointing authority, which would then appoint the tribunal if the parties cannot agree. (Possible appointing authorities include the Institution of Civil Engineers, the Institution of Chemical Engineers and the Institution of Electrical Engineers.)

In addition, the various engineering institutions also have their own sets of rules which are appropriate for disputes in particular disciplines, such as:

- the Institution of Chemical Engineers' Forms of Contract Arbitration Rules ('The Pink Book')
- the Institution of Civil Engineers' Arbitration Procedure (2006)
- the Society of Construction Arbitrators' Construction Industry Model Arbitration Rules (CIMAR).

Arbitration clause

Each of the arbitration institutions and the standard forms of contract recommend an appropriate form of wording, which should be used. However, the following considerations should be taken into account when finalising the exact form of the arbitration agreement.

(1) Parties should always consider what disputes they want to refer to arbitration and ensure that the clause is sufficiently wide to ensure that all disputes are properly referable to arbitration.
(2) Consideration must be given to a number of arbitrators. For smaller disputes, a sole arbitrator is normally sufficient. For larger or more complex disputes, a tribunal of three arbitrators is normal (for obvious reasons, it is best to have an odd number of arbitrators).
(3) The commonly used arbitration rules provide a comprehensive code for the appointment of arbitrators, including default provisions in the event that the parties cannot agree. If the parties wish an arbitrator to have certain professional attributes, this should be specifically stated. For example, 'a Chartered Engineer with at least 15 years experience in the oil and gas industry'.
(4) The place (or 'seat') of arbitration should be expressly stated. The place of arbitration has important ramifications for both the procedural law applicable to the arbitration (in England, the Arbitration Act 1996) and enforcement of the award (which should generally be a New York Convention country).
(5) For international disputes, it is important to state the language of arbitration to avoid the need for unnecessary duplication and translation of documentary and witness evidence.
(6) In some jurisdictions, such as England, there is a limited right of appeal to the courts which can be waived by the parties. Many of the institutional rules (such as ICC and LCIA) automatically waive that right of appeal, and the parties should decide whether they wish that to be the case or not.
(7) Finally, consideration must be given as to whether there are any particular mandatory requirements of the governing law of the place (or seat) of arbitration which need to be incorporated into the rules. Overseas contracts are often entered into with government departments or entities, so it is important to ensure that advice is taken on the effect of any state immunities or privileges which are enjoyed by such governmental bodies.

Commencing an arbitration

In litigation, a matter is commenced when a party issues a claim form in the relevant court upon payment of an appropriate fee (refer to

Chapter 4). An arbitration is commenced when one party issues a relevant notice of arbitration. This notice is important for three reasons:

(1) It defines the scope of the dispute between the parties and the matters which are to be referred to arbitration. It is therefore advisable to ensure that the notice of arbitration is drafted in wide terms so that all potential claims which a party might wish to make within the arbitration are included within the reference.

(2) It is important for limitation purposes, which are legal time bars that prevent a party from making claims after the expiration of a defined period of time. For example, under English law the limitation period for breach of contract is usually 6 years from the date of the breach of contract. The date upon which an arbitration is commenced stops the clock and is therefore of crucial importance if a party is close to the expiry of the relevant limitation period.

(3) If the notice of arbitration is improperly drafted, it might allow the defendant to avoid the reference to arbitration. Whilst such defects can often be cured by the serving of a compliant notice of arbitration, this is not possible if a limitation period has in the meantime expired. It is therefore important to ensure that a notice of arbitration is carefully and accurately drafted.

In order to decide how to commence an arbitration, a party should first refer to the terms of the contract and, in particular, the procedural rules applicable. Many of the institutional rules (such as the ICC and LCIA) prescribe the procedure which the parties must follow in order to commence an arbitration and specify when a matter is commenced for limitation purposes. (Refer to Chapter 10 for an example ICC request for arbitration.)

In the absence of a prescribed procedure, an arbitration under English law (in accordance with the Arbitration Act 1996) is commenced by one party serving a notice of dispute or notice of arbitration (they mean the same thing) on the other party and inviting the respondent to concur in the appointment of an arbitrator. Examples of a letter before action and a notice of arbitration are set out in Boxes 5.1 and 5.2, respectively.

Multi-party claims

Where disputes arise under a contract between two parties, the commencement and progress of an arbitration is relatively straightforward. However, construction projects often involve many parties with, typically, an employer, a main contractor and numerous subcontractors (and often numerous sub-subcontractors and subsuppliers). Where there are a number of parties and contracts, but all relating to the same project, it is sensible to execute a separate umbrella arbitration agreement allowing consolidation of disputes. Having a dispute determined by a single tribunal is beneficial in terms of cost and time efficiency, and also eliminates the risk of inconsistent findings.

Choosing an arbitration tribunal

The number of arbitrators is normally specified in the arbitration clause in the contract. If a contract is silent, the parties will need to consider

---

Box 5.1: Model letter before action

1st April 2005

Dear Sir

New Delhi Power Station Project

1. We are solicitors instructed by the Bavarian Power Company Ltd, the contractor engaged by your client (New Delhi Electricity Ltd) to supply, install and commission a new 240 megawatt generator in your client's existing power station.
2. The Contract between the parties is an amended version of the MF/1 Model Form of Contract for the supply of electrical or mechanical plant, with erection, produced by the Institution of Electrical Engineers and the Institution of Mechanical Engineers. By clause 40.1 hereof your client, the Purchaser under the Contract, is obliged to pay our client, the Contractor, the sum certified as due in a Certificate of Payment within 30 days after the date of issue thereof. We are instructed that Certificate No. 10 was issued and dated on 1st February 2005 but that your client has failed to pay the certified sum of US$100,000, notwithstanding that the prescribed payment period of 30 days has now long since past.
3. Accordingly, we hereby give you notice that if your client fails to make payment immediately (and in any event by no later than 8th April 2005) in accordance with the said clause 40, our client will be obliged to commence arbitration proceedings to recover the sums due.
4. Please acknowledge safe receipt of this letter.

Yours etc.

---

whether they wish to have the dispute determined by a sole arbitrator or by a tribunal (usually of three). In making that decision, the following points are relevant:

- Under most institutional rules, the preference is for a sole arbitrator unless the dispute is complex or of sufficient value to warrant a tribunal (in general, a dispute of more than £1,000,000 would warrant a tribunal).
- There is no reason in principle why even a high value and complex dispute cannot be decided by a sole arbitrator. Nevertheless, parties often perceive that a tribunal containing three members will give them a more balanced award.
- An arbitration before a tribunal is likely to take longer than one before a sole arbitrator, simply because of the need for the members of the tribunal to meet at periodic intervals to discuss the dispute and the need to co-ordinate three diaries for hearing dates with the parties.

Box 5.2: Model arbitration notice

Dear Sir

Arbitration Notice: Bavarian Power Company Ltd v. New Delhi Electricity Ltd

1. Please refer to our earlier letter before action, dated 1st April 2005. In that letter we gave your client notice that if they failed to honour the payment provision in clause 40.1 of the MF/1 Model Form of Contract (Rev. 4), 2000 Edition, produced by the IEE/IMechE, our client would be obliged to commence arbitration proceedings to recover the sums owing.

2. Since we and our client have received no response at all to the previous letter, please note that this letter is intended to constitute an Arbitration Notice for the purposes of clause 52.1 of the said Contract. For the avoidance of doubt, the dispute or difference which has arisen between the Purchaser (your client) and the Contractor (our client) is the failure by your client, in breach of Contract, to make payment, pursuant to clause 40.1, of the sum certified in Certificate No. 10 dated 1st February 2005, within 30 days of the date of issue thereof. Your client's failure continues, notwithstanding that the said 30 days payment period expired more than 2 months ago.

3. Accordingly, by this letter the said dispute or difference is hereby referred to arbitration by a person to be agreed upon. Failing agreement upon such person within 30 days after the date of this Notice, the arbitration shall be conducted by some person appointed on the application of either party by the President of the institution named in the appendix (namely: the Institution of Electrical Engineers, London).

4. In order to secure agreement with you as regards the identity of the proposed arbitrator, we now propose the following three persons for you to choose one. Alternatively please propose your own list of three names.

    (i) John Smith, FIEE, of (address);
    (ii) Alex Brown, of (address); and
    (iii) Peter Green, FIMechE, of (address).

5. Bearing in mind that clause 52.1 provides only 30 days for securing agreement upon the identify of an arbitrator, we would ask for your response to the above proposals within 7 days of the date of this letter. Further and in any event, we would ask for your immediate confirmation of safe receipt of this letter, which is being sent by recorded delivery.

Yours etc.

- For obvious reasons, a tribunal will be more expensive than a sole arbitrator and is therefore better suited to high-value disputes, where the tribunal's fees will be low in comparison with the overall sums in dispute.

Conducting an arbitration

As arbitration is flexible and informal, it is very much up to the parties and the tribunal to decide how to conduct the arbitration. Section 33 of the Arbitration Act 1996 sets out the general duties of the tribunal, and provides that it shall:

(1) act fairly and impartially between the parties, giving each party a reasonable opportunity of putting its case and dealing with that of its opponent, and
(2) adopt procedures suitable to the circumstances of the particular case, avoiding unnecessary delay or expense, so as to provide a fair means for the resolution of the matter to be determined.

One of the first steps in many arbitrations is for the tribunal to convene a procedural hearing, in which the parties discuss the matters in dispute, the timetable, the extent of the documentation and the need for witness evidence. The parties are often able to agree upon these matters, but in the event of disagreement it is for the tribunal to determine and fix the most appropriate procedure. Whilst every arbitration is different, there is a typical series of stages leading up to a hearing – these are set out in the following subsections.

Written submissions

The notice of arbitration is usually very brief and sets out in general terms the matters in dispute. It will therefore be necessary for parties to provide detailed written submissions outlining both the factual and legal bases of their respective positions. In litigation, these submissions are referred to as 'pleadings', and would be restricted to the essential legal and factual matters in dispute. In arbitration, submissions are typically more detailed, setting out the background to the dispute, the factual and legal issues, together with extracts from relevant documentation, which are often appended to the submissions themselves. In other words, the written submissions in arbitration are often intended to set out the entirety of each party's case.

Whilst the tribunal will give guidance as to the scope and extent of the submissions, a typical exchange would be as follows:

(1) Claimant: Statement of case.
(2) Respondent: Defence and counterclaim.
(3) Claimant: Reply and defence to counterclaim.
(4) Respondent: Reply to defence to counterclaim.

Documents

In litigation before the English courts, the parties have an obligation to provide the other party with copies of all documents relevant to the issues in dispute, a process referred to as 'disclosure' (see Chapter 4 for further details). In arbitration, the process of document disclosure is entirely different and, in many cases, misunderstood.

A common misconception is that by choosing to arbitrate a dispute in London, both parties will be entitled to extensive disclosure from the other party in a similar way that parties are entitled to disclosure in English court litigation. That is, however, not the case. It is entirely a matter for a tribunal to decide all evidential matters, including whether any, and if so which, documents or classes of documents should be disclosed (section 34(2)(d) of the Arbitration Act 1996). Therefore, the scope of the disclosure obligation on the parties will be determined by the tribunal, which underlines the importance of taking care in choosing the members of the tribunal. Whilst it is often the case that a tribunal of English lawyers will be more amenable to a wide disclosure of documents in arbitration, that is not always the case. If a party wishes to have the right to extensive disclosure, it should do so by providing an express right in the arbitration clause in the contract.

Factual witnesses

Virtually all disputes require witness evidence to bridge the gaps in the contemporaneous documentation and to set the whole dispute in context. Where particular agreements or discussions are not set out in correspondence, it is essential that the relevant witnesses give evidence as to what was said or done so that the tribunal can reach a decision.

Expert witnesses

Construction disputes often concern complex technical issues. These can include determining whether a particular design is wrong or whether the standard of workmanship is inadequate, and identifying responsibility for defects in the completed works.

For these reasons, it is very common in arbitrations for the parties to appoint their own experts, who provide reports and opinions on the technical matters in dispute. The purpose of these reports is to assist the tribunal in understanding the issues and reaching a decision on culpability. Whilst experts are appointed and paid by each respective party, their overriding duty is to the tribunal and so their reports should provide an impartial and independent opinion on the matters in dispute. In many cases, the entire dispute can turn upon a specific technical issue and so the choice of expert can be absolutely crucial.

In addition, a tribunal might appoint its own expert. This can happen when the parties do not think that the matters in dispute justify the appointment of separate experts, or where the tribunal feels that it needs help in understanding and distinguishing between two competing expert reports. Whilst tribunal-appointed experts can often be of invaluable assistance, care must be taken to ensure that the expert is not another unnecessary cost that does not help to narrow the issues or resolve the underlying dispute.

Typical arbitration timetable

Every arbitration is different. The timetable will depend upon the views of the tribunal, the conduct of the parties, the complexity of the matters in dispute and the time needed for the parties to develop their cases and be ready for a hearing. Nevertheless, set out below is a typical timetable for a large and complex construction dispute requiring factual and expert witness evidence:

Procedural hearing:	Month 1
Claimant's statement of case:	Month 3
Respondent's defence and counterclaim:	Month 5
Claimant's reply and defence to counterclaim:	Month 6
Respondent's reply to defence to counterclaim:	Month 7
Disclosure of documents:	Month 9
Exchange of witness statements:	Month 12
Exchange of experts' reports:	Month 14
Hearing:	Month 18
Award:	Month 20–24

A large and complex construction dispute can therefore take up to 2 years to resolve. Conversely, many smaller arbitrations are resolved in a matter of months, especially where there is limited documentary and expert evidence. The parties can also agree to dispose of certain matters without the need for an oral hearing, and can place restrictions on both the length and scope of witness evidence. As the parties have agreed to a private form of dispute resolution, it is up to the parties to follow a procedure that they both want, and at a speed that they want.

Ancillary relief

It is not uncommon for one of the parties to make applications to the tribunal for interim or ancillary relief. This can take many forms, but typically might be for:

- security for costs
- injunctive relief
- ordering samples to be taken or experiments to be carried out
- provisional orders for the payment of money.

Often, a reluctant respondent will seek to utilise some or all of the above items in an effort to slow down the progress of the arbitration and avoid an award against it. An experienced tribunal is normally alert to such tactical ploys and would ensure that the progress of the arbitration is not unduly delayed.

The arbitration hearing

At the hearing the parties make oral submissions, witnesses and experts are cross-examined and the tribunal can raise issues that it wants to have resolved. It allows each party to 'have its day in court'. However, an oral hearing is not always necessary nor appropriate, and consideration should be given as to whether there are more cost-effective ways to resolve the dispute.

Section 34(2)(h) of the Arbitration Act 1996 gives the tribunal a discretion to decide if and to what extent there should be oral evidence or submissions. As a general rule, where there is contested factual evidence of what was said or done, it will be necessary to have a hearing to allow the tribunal to judge the veracity of the witnesses and ascertain the true position. However, as many construction and engineering disputes do not depend upon factual evidence, there are other ways of determining the dispute without the need for a hearing:

- The tribunal could decide a dispute by relying on documents only. This approach might be appropriate when there is a dispute as to the scope of works set out in a specification attached to a contract, which the tribunal can determine based on a review of the specification alone.
- In disputes concerning defective work, it might well be sufficient for the tribunal to carry out a site visit, inspect the works for itself and reach its decision based on that inspection.
- Where a dispute concerns expert evidence, it is helpful for the experts to meet on a 'without prejudice' basis to try to narrow the issues between them, so that any hearing is limited to the remaining core matters in dispute between the parties and upon which the experts do not agree.

As the hearing is usually the most expensive part of the whole arbitration process, it is prudent and sensible to consider appropriate steps to limit both the length and scope of the hearing.

Preparation
In litigation, the building and facilities are provided and allocated by the court. In arbitration, everything has to be arranged by the parties or the tribunal, which can take a considerable time, especially in circumstances where one party is reluctant to agree to anything that incurs additional costs. Anyone organising an arbitration hearing should consider the following points:

- A venue, which needs to be agreed and booked, must include a room of sufficient capacity to hold the tribunal and representatives from both parties, together with witnesses, experts and documents.
- The place of arbitration is usually neutral to both parties, and therefore consideration needs to be given to retiring rooms, where each party can discuss the matter confidentially and prepare submissions or documents.
- It is common in complex arbitrations for a transcriber to be available to take a record of everything that is said during the course of the hearing, which is then typed up into a written document.
- The parties should agree upon a core bundle, which is essentially a series of files containing all the key documents that the parties propose to rely upon at the hearing. A clean copy of the core bundle will need to be provided for the witnesses giving evidence.

In respect of all these items, it is important to ensure that the basis upon which arrangements are made is clearly defined and cost responsibility agreed. Typically, the parties would agree to share the costs on a 50/50 basis until the tribunal issues its award, with any costs reallocated as appropriate.

Opening submissions
It is common for the parties to provide opening submissions at the beginning of a hearing. These can take the form of either written submissions sent to the tribunal prior to the hearing, or oral submissions made by each party at the hearing itself. The purpose of these submissions is to introduce and set out each party's case based on the documentary, factual and witness evidence already before the tribunal, so that the tribunal is able to focus on the key issues in dispute.

Hearing timetable
Arbitrators are busy practitioners and will only allocate a specific period of time for a hearing, and in some cases hearings will be held in several tranches. In both cases, it is up to the parties as to how to allocate the time so that it is used efficiently.

Closing submissions
Closing submissions draw together each party's case and include the oral evidence obtained from the hearing. These submissions are the last opportunities that the parties will have to make any points to the tribunal, but the parties should not raise any new issues, i.e. issues that have not already been addressed during the course of the hearing. As there is often a considerable amount of oral evidence at the hearing, there is a tendency for written closing submissions to be extremely long, especially where a transcript of the hearing is available. It is therefore not uncommon for tribunals to restrict the length of written closing submissions.

The arbitration award
A distinction should be drawn between the orders and directions of the tribunal adopted during the course of the arbitration, which address procedural matters, and an award, which is a final determination of a particular issue in dispute in the arbitration. This distinction is important because under the Arbitration Act 1996 it is possible for a party to challenge or appeal an award to the courts, but procedural orders or directions cannot be challenged.

Final award
The purpose of the tribunal's final award is to determine all the issues in dispute in the arbitration and provide a complete decision that is capable of enforcement without the need for further steps by the parties. Once the final award has been issued and there are no further matters to be decided, the tribunal's jurisdiction comes to an end and it is said to be 'functus officio'. The tribunal thereafter has no further power to hear the parties (except in a number of restricted circumstances, described in the section Challenging arbitration awards).

In accordance with section 58(1) of the Arbitration Act 1996, the award made by the tribunal is (unless otherwise agreed by the parties) final and binding. It is therefore conclusive in respect of the matters in dispute and, unless there is a successful challenge, can be enforced by either of the parties.

Although it is important for most parties to obtain a timely decision, there are no specific time limits by which tribunals should issue their awards. Article 24 of the ICC rules specifies a time limit of 6 months for final award from the signature of the terms of reference, but the tribunal is entitled to extend that time limit (which is more often the case than not). The parties are therefore reliant upon the diligence of the tribunal to produce a timely final award, which underlines the importance of selecting an appropriate tribunal at the start of the dispute.

Interest
Disputes are usually not referred to arbitration until well after a project is finished, and it may then take 1 to 2 years for a final award, resulting in one of the parties being kept out of its money for a considerable period of time. The tribunal is given power under section 49 of the Arbitration Act 1996 to award interest (subject to any contrary agreement by the parties). In particular, the tribunal can award simple or compound interest, from such dates and at such rates as it considers meet the justice of the case. The tribunal therefore has a fairly wide power to award interest, both in terms of the rate and the period. However, it must be remembered that interest should only compensate the winning party for having been kept out of its money, and not be a penal measure designed to punish the losing party.

The contract often provides a rate of interest, or alternatively the tribunal might adopt the prevailing bank rates or court rates over the relevant period. In some cases, it might be necessary for one party to demonstrate the actual cost of not having been paid the sum earlier by reference to its annual accounts and borrowing costs.

Costs
The parties can ask the tribunal to award costs or refer the question of costs to the court for determination. The costs are defined as:

(1) the arbitrator's fees and expenses
(2) the fees and expenses of any arbitral institution concerned
(3) the legal or other costs to the parties.

The first two categories are self-explanatory, but the third category is potentially very wide. This includes all costs reasonably and properly incurred by either party in presenting a case throughout the entirety of the arbitration proceedings, e.g. legal costs, expert's fees, and costs of other advisers engaged to assist with the preparation or conduct of the case. It is not uncommon for parties to seek to recover internal management costs on the basis that their employees would have been engaged in other productive work were it not for the need to spend time preparing for and assisting with the conduct of the arbitration.

The English-style approach that costs follow the event is preserved by the Arbitration Act 1996 (section 61), which allows the tribunal to make an award that allocates the costs of the arbitration between the parties and (unless the parties otherwise agree) on the general principle that costs follow the event.

The costs of the arbitration can easily exceed the sum in dispute, and consideration should therefore be given at an early stage to protect a party's costs position. There are numerous ways in which this can be done, but the parties should consider the following options:

- Persuade the tribunal to exercise its discretion to limit the amount of recoverable costs in advance of the arbitration process (section 65 of the Arbitration Act 1996).
- Put in what is called a 'sealed offer', which is the equivalent of making a payment into court. A sealed offer is usually stated to be expressed 'without prejudice save as to costs', and will make an offer to settle the matter for a certain sum. If a claimant fails to beat that sum, the defendant is entitled to its costs in any event.

The traditional approach of the courts to costs has been fairly restrictive, with the parties expecting to recover only 60 to 65% of their legal costs, with often little (if any) recovery for internal management costs. The Arbitration Act 1996 provides a much greater discretion to both the tribunal or the court to determine costs on such basis as it thinks fit. There is a growing tendency for tribunals to take account of the concept of proportionality, whereby costs are only considered to be reasonable if they are proportionate to the sums in dispute and the efforts necessary to conduct the arbitration in an efficient manner. Nevertheless, many arbitrators come from a commercial background and are familiar with the realities of funding and conducting litigation. Arbitrators therefore tend to be more generous in awarding the winning party its costs than might otherwise be the case if the matter were referred to detailed scrutiny by the courts.

Challenging arbitration awards

Once the tribunal has issued its final award and becomes *functus officio*, the reference terminates and the tribunal's authority is brought to an end. The award is final and binding, and can be enforced by any party through the courts in the event of non-compliance.

There are, nevertheless, three limited grounds under which the parties can seek to challenge the terms of the final award.

The 'slip' rule

The tribunal has a limited residual power to correct its final award if there is a clerical mistake or error arising from an accidental slip or omission or if it needs to clarify or remove any ambiguity (unless the parties have agreed otherwise – section 57 of the Arbitration Act 1996). Whilst many parties regularly attempt to use the slip rule to seek to persuade a tribunal to change its award entirely, the scope of the slip rule is limited to three particular situations:

(1) There is a clerical error, which often occurs when a tribunal makes an arithmetical mistake in adding up a series of numbers in a column.

(2) There is an error arising from an accidental slip or omission, which includes the situation whereby something was left out by accident or incorrectly inserted by the tribunal.

(3) To enable the tribunal to clarify or remove an ambiguity in its award. This would not involve making any change to the award itself, but rather clarifying what it meant by a particular phrase or term in the award.

Essentially, the rule allows the tribunal to correct minor slips or errors, but applications must generally be made within 28 days of the date of award and the slip rule is thus of only limited application.

Appeals

A party can try to appeal to the court on a question of law arising out of an arbitral award under section 69 of the Arbitration Act 1996, although it should be noted that the right to appeal can be excluded by the parties by agreement and many of the institutional rules (including the ICC and LCIA rules) waive that right of appeal.

Even if there is no exclusion of the right to appeal, a party has to obtain the permission of the court to proceed with an appeal. That permission is only granted if the court is satisfied that:

(1) the determination of the question will substantially affect the rights of one or more of the parties

(2) the question is one which the tribunal was asked to determine

(3) the basis of the findings of fact by the tribunal on the question is obviously wrong, or the question is one of general public importance and the decision of the tribunal is at least open to serious doubt, and

(4) it is just and proper in all the circumstances for the court to determine the question.

The practical reality of those provisions is that it is very difficult to persuade the court to grant a party permission to appeal an arbitration award on a question of law (the tribunal's findings of fact are conclusive and cannot be challenged). Appeals against arbitration awards issued in England are understandably rare.

Procedural irregularity

Finally, a party can apply to the court to challenge an award on the grounds of serious irregularity affecting the tribunal, the proceedings or the award, or where it is said that the tribunal had no substantive jurisdiction to determine the issues in dispute.

The right to challenge an award on the basis that there has been a serious irregularity in the arbitration process itself is really a safeguard. It is only exercised in extreme cases where the tribunal has made so serious a mistake in the conduct of the arbitration that the court should not stand by and let that injustice stand without correction. For the court to intervene (under section 68 of the Arbitration Act 1996), the irregularity has to have caused or will cause substantial injustice to one of the parties. Grounds giving rise to serious irregularity include issues such as fraud, failure by the tribunal to deal with all the issues that were put to it, conduct being contrary to public policy or the tribunal exceeding its powers.

The right to challenge an award for lack of substantive jurisdiction only arises once the tribunal has issued its final award, and a challenge is typically made on the basis that the arbitration agreement was invalid or that the tribunal issued a decision in respect of matters that were not within the scope of the arbitration or the agreement to arbitrate. A challenge must be made promptly – a party can lose the right to object by taking part in the arbitration without making a timely objection (section 67 of the Arbitration Act 1996).

Summary

Arbitration is a private form of dispute resolution which is an alternative procedure to public litigation in the courts. The private and confidential nature of arbitration makes it attractive to many commercial organisations as the preferred method for resolving their disputes. It is particularly appropriate for international disputes, where enforcement is important.

6. Adjudication

Samuel Townend

Introduction

Adjudication is one of the array of dispute resolution procedures available to disputing parties in the construction industry. It is typically a time- and cost-limited procedure often exercised during the course of a construction contract, and it is aimed at delivering certainty on the particular point between the parties while leaving open the possibility of subsequent debate in a more deliberative and thorough manner at a later stage by way of arbitration or litigation. [A characteristic of adjudication is that the decision on the issue in dispute is made by a third party, who is usually not involved in the day-to-day operation of the contract and is not an arbitrator or a judge.]

Adjudication has long been part of the panoply of alternative dispute resolution procedures available to parties to construction contracts, but until recent years it was far from universal and, if the case law that refers to it is anything to go by, was not greatly utilised. Where it was adopted by the parties, it was by express agreement in writing and was based on an ad hoc set of rules (which differed from contract to contract). A decision reached by an adjudicator was then given whatever effect had previously been agreed by the parties in the contract, whether to be a final and binding decision or of temporary effect only. The precise effect of the adjudicator's decision, the procedure to be adopted, the appointment of the adjudicator and the costs of the adjudication were all matters that had to be agreed by the parties prior to contract. Contractual adjudication found a place in some standard forms of building contract, such as the JCT Standard Form of Building Contract with Contractor's Design 1981 as amended in 1988, in which adjudication was introduced by the provision of supplementary provisions. This was, however, relatively unusual and it was not until the coming into force of the Housing Grants, Construction and Regeneration Act 1996 (referred to here as the 'Construction Act') that adjudication became commonplace. Since then, knowledge of adjudication and how it can be used by a party to a construction contract has been essential for any engineer playing a certifying, advisory or commercial role in a construction contract.

The Construction Act and the Scheme

The provision of statutory or compulsory adjudication together with other substantive measures by the Construction Act was the government's response to a perception that contractors in the construction industry needed a legislative helping hand in avoiding problems, in particular those associated with difficulties with cash flow, which was causing so many of them to fold prematurely. There was a perception that many employers (developers, financiers and main contractors) were using their superior commercial power to process payment applications slowly, or even withhold sums otherwise properly due until they themselves were paid. The provisions of the Construction Act were aimed at limiting those cash-flow difficulties by, for example, banning 'pay when paid' clauses and by statutory implication providing for adjudication as a dispute resolution procedure in every construction contract.

A useful description of statutory adjudication was given by the judge who presided over the first case concerning adjudication which came to court, Dyson J (*Macob Civil Engineering Ltd* v. *Morrison Construction Ltd* [1999] BLR at paragraph 24):

> The intention of Parliament in enacting the Act was plain. It was to introduce a speedy mechanism for settling disputes in construction contracts on a provisional interim basis, and requiring the decision of adjudicators to be enforced pending the final determination of disputes by arbitration, litigation or agreement... The timetable for adjudications is very tight... Many would say unreasonably tight, and likely to result in injustice. Parliament must be taken to have been aware of this. So far as procedure is concerned, the adjudicator is given a fairly free hand. It is true (but hardly surprising) that he is required to act impartially... He is, however, permitted to take the initiative in ascertaining the facts and the law... He may, therefore, conduct an entirely inquisitorial process, or he may, as in the present case, invite representations from the parties. It is clear that Parliament intended that the adjudication should be conducted in a manner which those familiar with the grinding detail of the traditional approach to the resolution of construction disputes apparently find difficult to accept. But Parliament has not abolished arbitration and litigation of construction disputes. It has merely introduced an intervening provisional stage in the dispute resolution process. Crucially, it has made it clear that the decisions of adjudicators are binding and are to be complied with until the dispute is finally resolved.

Adjudication was intended to mark a sea change in how parties to construction contracts resolve matters in dispute between them, and it does appear to have had that effect.

Application of statutory adjudication
Statutory adjudication applies to construction contracts in England, Wales and Scotland as defined in section 104 of the Construction Act. There are some limitations to the application of statutory adjudication – it does not apply to every contract under which construction activities are to take place.

Construction contracts to which the Construction Act and statutory adjudication applies include contracts for the carrying out of construction operations or the arranging for the carrying out of construction operations. Also included are contracts to do architectural, design or surveying work, or to provide advice on building, engineering, interior or exterior decoration or on the laying-out of landscape, so long as in relation to construction operations. Specifically excluded from the ambit of the Construction Act are contracts where the work is for the extraction of oil, gas or minerals, most work associated with the assembly, installation or demolition of plant or machinery on sites where the primary activity is nuclear processing, power generation, water or effluent treatment, production and processing of chemicals, pharmaceuticals, oil, gas, steel or food and drink. Also excluded are the simple manufacture and supply of materials, plant or machinery. Simple sale-of-goods contracts do not fall within the Construction Act. Similarly, where the contract is with a residential occupier the provisions of the Construction Act do not apply. These are the main exclusions; however, the Construction Act should be checked for a comprehensive list of the excluded activities.

In order for statutory adjudication to apply, the construction contract must also be in writing or evidenced in writing (section 107(2)). This is quite a technical matter and the precise extent of the requirement for writing has been the subject of debate before the courts, however a general proposition is of utility – that if all the relevant terms are set out in writing this will usually be sufficient.

The key characteristic of adjudication provided for under the Construction Act is that any party to a construction contract may refer a dispute arising under the contract for adjudication at any time. It is not possible to contract out of this or other aspects of statutory adjudication – the contract must provide for adjudication at any time. In other words, no conditions may be placed in a construction contract as to when a party may seek an adjudicator's decision on a point in dispute. Any contract terms that state that there is a requirement for the parties to mediate or have a meeting of directors before they have a right to refer a matter to adjudication will be of no effect.

The Construction Act also provides for other mandatory provisions concerning adjudication which, if any of them are absent from the written terms of the contract, the adjudication provisions of the Scheme for Construction Contracts apply (referred to here as 'the Scheme'). The Scheme is a set of regulations issued shortly after the Construction Act came into force. The provisions of the Scheme replace wholesale the non-conforming adjudication provisions provided in the contract. To avoid the imposition of the Scheme, the contract must provide for access to adjudication at any time and:

(1) require the appointment of an adjudicator and receipt by the adjudicator of a referral notice (a document containing details of the claim) within 7 days of the claiming party (usually referred to as the 'referring party'), giving the other party (usually referred to as the 'responding party') notice of their intention to refer a dispute to adjudication

(2) require that the adjudicator should reach a decision within 28 days of referral, to be capable of extension for up to 14 days with

the agreement of just the referring party and the adjudicator. (It is worth noting that this timetable is markedly short for those familiar with the lengthy processes of orthodox construction dispute resolution. This has the great benefit to the parties of limiting the costs to be paid to lawyers, claims consultants and experts. It is, however, perhaps absurdly short for a dispute concerning a complex delay and disruption claim which has arisen over a substantial period of time. It is always open for the parties and the adjudicator in given cases to agree to extend time for as long as they all wish.)

(3) provide that the adjudicator acts impartially – the rules of natural justice apply to the extent permitted by the statutorily limited timetable

(4) provide that the adjudicator may take the initiative in ascertaining the facts and the law – in other words, the adjudicator chooses and directs the procedure to be adopted subject to the general framework provided by the Construction Act

(5) provide for the adjudicator to be immune from any subsequent claim made against him or her for any act or omission in the conduct of the adjudication unless done in bad faith, and

(6) require that the decision of the adjudicator is binding until the dispute is finally determined by legal proceedings, by arbitration or by agreement.

This last point is the one that gives statutory adjudication its teeth and is the reason why adjudication must be taken seriously by all parties. The courts have been rigorous in enforcing the decisions of adjudicators in accordance with this requirement, whether or not they agreed with the adjudicator's factual or legal reasoning or conclusions. The reason for this was explored by His Honour Judge Lloyd in his judgment in *Outwing* v. *Randall* [1999] BLR 156 at 160:

Parliament intended that adjudicator's decisions and orders, if not complied with, were to be enforced without delay. It is clear that the purpose of the Act is that disputes are resolved quickly and effectively and then put to one side and revived, if at all, in litigation or arbitration, the hope being that the decision of the adjudicator might be accepted or form the basis of a compromise or might usefully inform the parties as to the possible reaction of the ultimate tribunal.

An adjudication decision will be enforceable irrespective of challenges to the merits or underlying validity of the adjudicator's decision. Effectively, there is no right of appeal to an adjudication decision. In practice it is noteable that there is seldom litigation or arbitration on matters which have already been adjudicated, although this is probably for reasons of the cost of carrying out further dispute resolution procedures as much as anything else. Adjudication is therefore a powerful tool for a party who is properly geared up for the rigours of what is a swift, rough-and-ready dispute resolution procedure.

The technical use of adjudication

Engineers advising employers or developers should be particularly careful about the technical use of adjudication by a contractor or subcontractors using other provisions in the Construction Act as to when sums are deemed payable to secure payment of sums irrespective of the presence of set-offs or counterclaims (such as defects in the works). Disputes put to an adjudicator for decision can be carefully identified and circumscribed by the referring contractor so as to preclude any substantial defence by the responding employer. This is sometimes described as an 'ambush', for obvious reasons.

To understand how an 'ambush' adjudication may happen it is necessary, briefly, to refer to other statutorily implied contract terms arising from the Construction Act particularly relating to payment.

Instalments

Apart from short-term construction contracts, of less than 45 days duration, the Construction Act requires that a contractor is entitled to payment by instalments. The employer and contractor are free to agree the amounts of the payments and the intervals at which, or circumstances in which, they become due. However, in the absence of such agreement the relevant provisions of the Scheme apply.

Where the parties have failed to agree the intervals by which instalments should be paid the Scheme provides that a stage payment becomes due simply on the making of a claim by the contractor. This can, of course, cause an employer great difficulties with cash flow, so an engineer advising an employer prior to agreement of a contract should always advise the employer to agree the intervals by which payments are to be made, and normally that they be lengthy periods.

The Construction Act further provides that every construction contract shall provide a final date for payment in relation to any sum that becomes due. The employer and contractor are also free to agree the final date for payment. In the absence of such agreement the Scheme again steps in, requiring payment to be made, at the latest, 17 days from the date the payment becomes due. In other words, where the parties have failed to agree any provisions as to payment instalments, a sum claimed by a contractor can be finally due just 17 days after the contractor simply makes a claim. An engineer advising prior to contract would be wise to suggest to the employer a longer period for the final date for payment.

There are also provisions as to when the final instalment falls due, namely the later of 30 days following completion of the work or the making of a claim by the contractor. Again, in all probability the employer would be better advised to agree up-front a longer period or breathing space before payment of the final instalment in order properly to assess the quality of the contractor's work, and the employer should ensure that the provisions for retention, if any, are fully integrated with the provision for final payment.

Notices

The Construction Act also requires an employer to respond actively and promptly to claims made by contractors and imposes a system of notices on an employer. The employer should be alert to the very quick responses required by the Construction Act.

First, the Construction Act provides that the employer should provide what has become known as a 'section 110 notice' to the contractor not later than 5 days from when the payment in relation to a particular claim becomes due. The section 110 notice should set out how much the employer proposes to pay and the basis upon which the amount is calculated.

Second, and more important, if the employer intends to withhold payments and not pay the whole of a contractor's application or claim, the employer must serve within time what has become known as a 'withholding notice'. This is provided for in section 111(1) of the Construction Act:

> A party to a construction contract may not withhold payment after the final date for payment of a sum due under the contract unless he has given an effective notice of intention to withhold payment.

To be effective this notice must specify the amount which is to be withheld and the ground or grounds for withholding payment. If more than one ground is cited the notice must also specify the amount of money attributable to each ground. A valid withholding notice must also be issued by the employer 'before the prescribed period', a period of time before the final date for payment. The parties are free to agree what the prescribed period is to be, and again the engineer when advising the employer prior to agreeing a construction contract should agree a short period prior to the final date for payment; alternatively, the terms of the Scheme step in, which require that a withholding notice must be given not later than 7 days before the final date for payment.

The section 110 notice may double as a withholding notice so long as it contains the required detail. It is certainly simpler to advise the employer to consider what its position will be on payment well before the deadline for service of a withholding notice.

The most concerning aspect for an employer in a contract to which the Construction Act applies is that if no agreement as to instalment payments or the notices mentioned above is made at the time of contracting it will be the case that just 10 days following the making of a claim, in the absence of a conforming withholding notice, the sum claimed by the contractor is due and the employer is not permitted to make any set-off or counterclaim.

Ambush adjudications or suspension of work
This is the principal advantage of the Construction Act to contractors. Contractors often exercise the right, where a sum due under a construction contract is not paid in full by the final date for payment and in the absence of an effective withholding notice, to pursue the employer for the full sum in an adjudication or to suspend work on the contract lawfully (section 112). This latter course of action is permitted subject only to the contractor giving the employer at least 7 days notice of intention to suspend and setting out the ground or grounds for suspension in the notice. A suspension by the contractor will be lawful (and not amount

to a repudiation of the contract) even where the employer has a valid set-off, if it has not been raised in a valid withholding notice. The right of the contractor to suspend work only ends when the employer makes payment in full of the amount deemed due.

There can be great advantages for the contractor in referring a technical dispute arising out of the Construction Act to an adjudication. Provided that the contractor has complied with such contractual procedures as there are for making payment applications, where there is no withholding notice issued by the employer, the application or invoice is deemed due for payment in full, and there is little scope for a defence by the employer if the adjudication notice (the document by which a party invokes an adjudication) is sufficiently narrowly worded. The employer may well not be able to raise a counterclaim or set-off in the adjudication in connection with, for example, manifest defects in the works.

Engineers' fees

It is worth noting that engineers, along with other construction professionals, can use the adjudication provisions in the Construction Act in much the same way as contractors to secure payment of their own fees arising out of any appointment they have relating to construction operations. The authority for this proposition is the case of *Gillies Ramsay Diamond* v. *PJW Enterprises Ltd* [2002] CILL 1901, in which the Scottish Court of Session decided that a letter containing conditions of appointment of a contract administrator was a construction contract under the Construction Act. This applies also to appointments as consultant to an employer or contractor.

Rules of adjudication

Beyond containing all of the express requirements set out in the previous sections, the rules and process of an adjudication may differ from contract to contract. As described above, in the absence of provisions for adjudication the rules in the Scheme apply (Section 109(3), Construction Act). Adjudication is generally a relatively informal process by which the adjudicator takes the initiative in establishing the facts of a case before coming to a decision. Experience tells that the vague nature of the procedure may, on occasion, and particularly in relation to a more complex dispute, lead to an unsatisfactory process where the parties' expectations as to how a matter is to proceed are not met. It may be useful for an advising engineer prior to agreement of the construction contract to suggest to the employer that provision is made in the contract for further and additional rules of adjudication to ensure that all sides know what they can expect and what they need to do in an adjudication should the right to have a matter decided in adjudication be invoked.

Presently, five industry bodies have produced and published adjudication rules:

- the Construction Industry Council (CIC) – CIC Model Adjudication Procedure (now in a third edition)

- the Centre for Dispute Resolution (CEDR) – CEDR Rules for Adjudication
- the Institution of Civil Engineers (ICE) – ICE Adjudication Procedure (1997)
- the Institution of Chemical Engineers (IChemE) – Forms of Contract Adjudication Rules ('The Grey Book', second edition)
- the Technology and Construction Solicitors Association (TeCSA) – TeCSA Adjudication Rules, 2002 version.

In addition, many standard forms of construction contract make detailed provision for the process of adjudication. One concern may be the cost of the procedure. The TeCSA Rules are the only ones which specify a cap on the amount that an adjudicator can charge and preclude the adjudicator from requiring advance payment or security. As a generalisation, the rules contained in standard forms of construction contract differ from the stand-alone rules. The former tend to specify the procedure and timetable to a greater degree, for example the JCT forms, the GC/Works and the NEC Engineering and Construction Contract all provide for provision of a response by the responding party in a given time.

The adjudication notice
The adjudication notice (or notice of adjudication) is the document which is the first step in initiating an adjudication. The two purposes of the adjudication notice are to inform the responding party of the intention to refer a dispute to an adjudicator and to identify and crystallise the dispute being referred. The notice of adjudication, either solely or together with the referral notice, prescribes the matters on which the adjudicator is to make a decision. It defines the jurisdiction of the adjudicator.

Different construction contracts and adjudication rules differently provide what should be contained in the adjudication notice. The Scheme requires the nature and brief description of the dispute to be set out and includes various other requirements. The JCT standard-form contracts require only that the notice briefly identifies the dispute or difference.

In any event, the adjudication notice needs to be drafted very carefully so as to avoid unnecessary disputes about the nature and extent of what has been referred to the adjudicator for decision.

As described above, carefully drafted adjudication notices can limit the extent to which a responding party may bring defences to the claim being made. To illustrate this, the following are two examples of a description of dispute in a notice of adjudication. The first is a narrow dispute where the adjudicator's jurisdiction is limited to deciding whether or not a particular invoice is due (perhaps taking advantage of the fact that no withholding notice has been served in time), and the second is a wider dispute which will require the adjudicator to investigate the true value of the works carried out:

(1) Whether E Employer do pay C Contractor the sum of £20,000 as per C's invoice dated 1st November 2005.
(2) What is C Contractor owed by E Employer under their building contract dated 1st July 2005?

An example of a fully detailed adjudication notice taking a withholding notice point is given in Box 6.1. It should be noted again that the minimum content of an adjudication notice may be determined by the adjudication provisions in the contract or the applicable adjudication rules. Careful attention should be paid to these when drawing up the adjudication notice and more, rather than less, information ought to be included to

---

Box 6.1: Example of an adjudication notice

IN THE MATTER OF AN ADJUDICATION

BETWEEN:

C CONTRACTOR LTD

Referring Party

– and –

E EMPLOYER LTD

Responding Party

ADJUDICATION NOTICE

1. This is a notice of the intention of the referring party ('C Ltd') to refer to adjudication a dispute with the responding party ('E Ltd'), pursuant to [clause x of the contract between them dated [y] [section 108 of the Housing Grants, Construction and Regeneration Act 1996].

Parties

2. The parties to the dispute are:

    (i) Referring party:

    C Contractor Ltd

    [Insert address]

    (ii) Responding party

    E Employer Ltd

    [Insert address]

The Dispute

3. The dispute between C Ltd and E Ltd arises out of a construction contract in writing between the parties dated [y] for the refurbishment of Hugh Gaitskell House, 22 High Street, Crawley. A copy of the contract is attached at appendix 1.
4. On 1st January payment application No. 10 was made by C Ltd to E Ltd in the sum of £100,000. There being no provision in the contract for payment terms the relevant provisions of the Scheme for Construction Contracts apply. The sum claimed by C Ltd therefore became due on 1st January.
5. 18th January was the final date for payment. No withholding notice having been issued on or before 11th January the responding party may not withhold payment after 18th January.
6. On 20th January C Ltd again applied to E Ltd for payment on application No. 10, but to date no payment has been made.
7. A dispute has therefore arisen. The adjudicator is asked to decide the following:

   7.1 that E Ltd do pay C Ltd the sum of £100,000 as per C Ltd's payment application No. 10 dated 1st January;
   7.2 that E Ltd do pay all the adjudicator's fees.

Signed......................   Dated.........................

ensure that the requirements of the agreed rules are met. If in doubt, guidance should be sought from someone with experience in drafting such documents, such as specialist solicitors or barristers or experienced claims consultants.

Appointment of an adjudicator

There are two principal ways in which an adjudicator may be identified and appointed:

(1) The adjudicator may be named in the contract or otherwise agreed prior to the dispute arising.
(2) The adjudicator is agreed by the parties following a dispute coming into being.

Appointment prior to the dispute

The advantage of this approach is that it saves time and acrimony in the identification and appointment process. On a dispute arising the process can be started by simply referring the dispute to the named adjudicator. Agreeing the identity of the adjudicator beforehand should give parties more confidence in the whole procedure and may reduce the chances of the losing party resisting the enforcement of a decision made by the named adjudicator.

A difficulty may arise, however, if the named adjudicator is unavailable. This can be overcome by naming more than one adjudicator in the contract, although this may lead to some dispute between the parties as to which of them should be chosen. A default procedure ought to be provided for if the named adjudicator or adjudicators are not available.

Named adjudicators may also, ultimately, lead to problems concerning the requirement that the adjudicator be impartial. There is no provision of independence. Thus, in theory, even an individual who is often employed by one party can, if impartial, act as an adjudicator. In practice it is hard to see how such an approach would have the confidence of both parties and may provide grounds (so long as accompanied with some substantive material) for the losing party to argue that the adjudicator did not act impartially in making his or her decision and therefore that the decision has no validity.

Appointment once dispute has arisen
Rather than naming an agreed individual, an appointing body may be named in the contract to appoint the adjudicator in the event of a dispute arising. It is also always useful to have provision of a method for appointment of an adjudicator in default of a named adjudicator being unavailable or the parties failing to agree. If the Scheme applies, in the absence of any provision for the adjudicator to be appointed by a named appointing body, the adjudicator shall be appointed by an 'adjudicator nominating body' on application by the referring party. An adjudicator nominating body is a body 'which holds itself out publicly as a body which will select an adjudicator when requested to do so by a referring party' (paragraph 2(3) of the Scheme). This is widely worded and there are a host of such bodies, ranging from the President of the Royal Institution of Chartered Surveyors (RICS) to the Chairman of the Technology and Construction Bar Association (TECBAR) to commercial bodies who are prepared to appoint (usually one of their own members) for the payment of a modest fee. All of the engineering professional bodies hold themselves out as adjudicator nominating bodies. Contact details for some other adjudicator nominating bodies are given in Box 6.2.

There is no generic format for an application to a body for appointment of an adjudicator. The adjudicator nominating bodies, particularly institutional and commercial ones, often have their own forms that they normally require to be filled in. Sometimes a degree of information about the dispute is requested to allow them to place the dispute with suitable individuals, including details of the value of the claim and the subject matter.

The referral notice
The referral notice is the document which contains all the information which the referring party wants to put to the adjudicator in order for the adjudicator to make his or her decision. The purpose is, of course, to persuade the adjudicator to make a decision in the referring party's favour. The contents of the referral notice should all be drafted with that aim in mind.

Box 6.2: Adjudicator nominating bodies

CEDR Dispute Resolution Service
Centre for Effective Dispute Resolution
International Dispute Resolution Centre
70 Fleet Street
London EC4Y 1EU
Tel. 0207 536 6001

The Chartered Institute of Arbitrators
International Arbitration Centre
12 Bloomsbury Square
London WC1A 2LP
Tel. 0207 421 7444

Clerk to the Chairman
The Technology and Construction Bar Association
Keating Chambers
15 Essex Street
London WC2R 3AA
Tel. 0207 544 2600

The Technology and Construction Solicitors' Association
Caroline Cummins
Chairwoman
TeCSA
C/o CMS Cameron McKenna
Mitre House, 160 Aldersgate Street
London EC1A 4DD

The referral notice is not like a legal pleading – it is more like a sub-mission in arbitration and can be relatively informal. When considering style and content the particular experience of the adjudicator should be borne in mind and the referral notice tailored accordingly.

Essential requirements of a referral notice include the following:

(1) There should be a re-statement of the dispute identified in the adjudication notice. Care should be taken not to expand the scope of the adjudication and therefore the jurisdiction of the adjudicator by making submissions on points that are not identified in the adjudication notice or which do not need to be addressed in order for the adjudicator to reach the decision sought. Any sub-issues that arise should be precisely identified.
(2) There should be a complete explanation of the claim. It will be for the referring party to prove its case on the balance of probabilities, thus it is important that the referral notice fully sets out the basis of the claim, normally being:

(i)   identification of the parties
(ii)   the contract
(iii) relevant contract documents
(iv)   the relevant terms of the contract
(v)   what obligations the responding party is said not to have complied with and how, and
(vi)   what loss has been caused to the referring party and how the loss has been caused together with the calculation of the loss.

(3) In the case of each of the above elements of the claim, documentation will be needed to prove the case, perhaps with witness statements from relevant individuals who can explain the case by reference to the documents. Contemporaneous documents should be used wherever possible and are preferred to documents generated for the purposes of the adjudication (though these may be necessary, for example a schedule of the calculation of the interest claim) together with the witness statements. These documents should be identified within and be appended to the referral notice.
(4) Any points of law that arise should be addressed expressly in the referral notice.
(5) At the end of the referral notice it may be useful to summarise the answers to each of the sub-issues referred for decision to provide the adjudicator with an agenda for the decision and which can double up as draft answers for incorporation in that decision should the adjudicator be persuaded.

Bearing in mind that this may be the only opportunity that the referring party has to make out its case it will usually also be necessary to deal, at least to some degree, with the matters of costs and meetings with the adjudicator.

Costs/offers
Costs are differentiated into the adjudicator's fees and ancillary costs of the adjudicator and each party's costs of participation in the adjudication. As stated above, provision is usually made in adjudication rules and the standard forms of construction contracts for the adjudicator to decide who should pay the adjudicator's costs. Paragraph 25 of the Scheme, for example, entitles the adjudicator to payment of a reasonable amount by way of fees and expenses reasonably incurred as determined by the adjudicator. The adjudicator is also entitled to determine how the payment is to be apportioned between the parties.

Each party's costs of participating in the adjudication are typically either not dealt with by the Construction Act, the Scheme or other rules, or the rules expressly provide that each party should bear its own costs. These amount to the same thing. In the ordinary case, therefore, each party will bear its own costs. In relation to most construction contracts, parties' costs will only be payable where the parties agree to confer jurisdiction on the adjudicator to award costs. In his judgment in *Northern Developments* v. *J & J Nichol* [2002] BLR 158 at 166, His Honour Judge Bowsher QC confirmed that there was no express or implied power in the Construction Act or Scheme for an adjudicator to decide that one party should pay the other party's costs. In this case both parties asked the adjudicator in writing for their costs. HHJ Bowsher QC construed this as an implied agreement to give the adjudicator jurisdiction to decide on costs.

Given the inherent strategic advantages to the referring party in adjudications, not least the ability to decide the scope of the matters to be decided in the adjudication and to limit the extent of defences that the responding party may bring, it will only be in very unusual cases that the responding party decides to confer jurisdiction upon the adjudicator to decide the parties' costs. Conversely, if confident of the case the referring party may well wish to confer jurisdiction on the adjudicator to award party costs. If advising the referring party, it is often worth trying to get an award of party costs. Otherwise, these costs will never be recovered.

Request for a meeting or a hearing

If the subject matter of the dispute is complicated or for some other reason a face-to-face meeting is thought useful (often where witness statements are relied upon), this should be requested in the referral notice. An adjudicator will often, but not always, call a meeting in any event. Where desired, an express request should be made to ensure that it happens.

Responding to adjudication proceedings

If responding to adjudication proceedings, it is most important that wherever possible the reference to adjudication is anticipated and that on receipt of an adjudication notice resources are immediately deployed and work begun on a response. As stated above, 'ambush' adjudications are commonplace, made worse when proceedings are issued over holiday periods such as August and Christmas. Notwithstanding the inconvenience, the adjudication proceedings must be taken seriously because although their effect is only temporarily binding, any decision will have effect until the end of a trial or arbitration, which may be as long as years after the adjudication decision. Further, statistically, adjudication decisions are determinative, not only because of the reluctance of the losing party to incur the immense further cost of litigating the matters in dispute, but also because the adjudication decision is often fairly taken as an impartial indication of how a court or tribunal will be likely to make judgment or award.

Before formulating a response to referral it is important to understand the precise extent of the dispute that is brought to adjudication. A responding party should ensure that the dispute referred is clear and unambiguous. If it is not, clarification should be sought. Often pressing for clarification of an ambiguous dispute might also give grounds for seeking an extension of time pending the clarification. This might not, of course, be granted (see below). Whether or not clarification is given it is useful to re-state the dispute and then press for agreement to the re-statement.

Any jurisdictional points should be registered as soon as they are identified and they should be maintained throughout the participation in the process. (Jurisdictional points are dealt with in the 'Enforcement' section of this chapter.) Essentially they are the only grounds upon which a losing party in an adjudication can resist in court the enforcement of the decision by the successful party. The responding party should not make the error of asking the adjudicator to decide on the jurisdictional points because asking the adjudicator to decide such a matter brings the whole issue within the adjudicator's jurisdiction and as a result there can be no appeal from any decision on jurisdiction reached by the adjudicator. This is coupled with the phenomenon that almost invariably the adjudicator, will decide that he or she has jurisdiction, as if there is not jurisdiction then that is the end of the adjudication (and there may even be a dispute about who will pay the adjudicator's costs). This is an unattractive consequence for the adjudicator, who will usually seek to avoid it where at all possible. For the avoidance of doubt, the rest of the response and continued participation in the adjudication should expressly be stated as being without prejudice to the primary contention that the adjudicator has no jurisdiction, and it should be stated that jurisdiction is not being conferred on the adjudicator to rule on any jurisdiction issue. The jurisdiction points should be included at least in summary form even though the adjudicator is not being asked to decide them. Notwithstanding what is stated above, there is always a slender chance that the adjudicator might nevertheless resign.

The form and contents of a response are not prescribed. In fact most adjudication rules (in contrast to most standard forms of construction contract) do not even refer to provision of a response let alone the format of it. If the adjudicator is to be impartial, however, it is thought that the responding party must be given an opportunity to provide a response. Experience tells that this will invariably be given.

Obtaining an extension of time

The referring party will have had many weeks or months within which to prepare the adjudication notice and referral notice. The responding party will normally only have a share of the time in the 28 days usually provided for within which to prepare and issue a response. As stated above, many standard form construction contracts provide for the responding party to provide a response to referral within 7 days of receipt of the referral notice or some other short period. The Scheme is silent as to a response or the time for provision of any response. Particularly in the more complicated cases, it is often a relatively simple task for the responding party to procure an extension of time from the adjudicator of up to about a further 7 days for service of the response because the adjudicator usually has unfettered discretion to direct what the parties do in the 28-day period typically allowed for the adjudicator to reach a decision.

A more substantial extension of time will be difficult to procure because under most rules the referring party holds all the cards in terms of allowing extension of time. Under the Construction Act one of the required terms of any construction contract is that the adjudication rules make provision for the referring party and adjudicator together to agree to a 14-day extension of time to the 28-day period. It is always open to the parties together with the adjudicator to agree an extension of time of any period. This often happens where the adjudicator requests additional time in order to complete the decision as neither party will want to risk upsetting the adjudicator.

If the nature and extent of the dispute is changed or clarified, that may also give a good reason by which to persuade the adjudicator of the need for an extension of time to allow for provision of the response. Once the adjudicator is persuaded and states so in writing the referring party may then be persuaded to agree to an extension of time.

In the context of some complicated final account disputes or delay and disruption disputes it may be worth trying out an argument that the adjudicator cannot, within the 28-day period allowed, come to a decision which is 'impartial' (as required in the Construction Act) or a decision which is not in breach of natural justice. In making out this argument reference may be made to the judgment of His Honour Judge Coulson QC, in the case of *William Verry (Glazing Systems) Ltd* v. *Furlong Homes Ltd* [2005] EWHC 138, (2005) CILL 2205 (at paragraph 11), where he expressly disapproves of the referral of complex final account disputes to adjudication:

> it [the notice of adjudication] referred to adjudication the entirety of the dispute about the Verry final account figure. This meant that Furlong wanted the adjudicator, during the statutory twenty-eight days, to reach decisions about disputed variations, extensions of time, loss expense and liquidated damages. In other words, all the potential disputes which can arise under a Building Contract were here being referred to adjudication. There was no express limitation or qualification on the range of matters for decision. It was, to use the vernacular, a 'kitchen sink' final account adjudication. Whilst such adjudications are not expressly prohibited by the Housing Grants, Construction and Regeneration Act 1996 as it presently stands, there is little doubt that composite and complex disputes such as this cannot easily be accommodated within the summary procedure of adjudication. A referring party should think very carefully before using the adjudication process to try and obtain some sort of perceived tactical advantage in final account negotiations and, in so doing, squeezing a wide-ranging final account dispute into a procedure for which it is fundamentally unsuited.

[emphasis added]

Substantive contents of a response

The substantial part of the response will deal with the substantive dispute contained in the adjudication notice and referral notice. Again, as stated above, prior to formulating the answers to the claims made it is useful to identify with precision the issues and sub-issues referred. This can act as a checklist when putting together the response.

Typically the response will be a similar document to the referral notice. It will address all of the points referred in an informal submission, making reference where useful to attached documents and witness statements. If the responding party disputes any of the points in the referral notice, it is important that the issues disputed are set out clearly. In every case the responding party should provide reasons for disputing a matter raised and supply any evidence in support. In addition, the scope of the adjudication permitting, any positive points in defence should be made out in the response. It is necessary to stress that this response may be the only opportunity the responding party will have to put its case to the adjudicator.

As with the referral notice, this submission should also deal with whether a hearing or meeting is useful and the responding party's case on costs.

Subsequent procedures

Due to the fact that adjudication may be an inquisitorial process and because all adjudication rules are completely silent on what happens between the response to a referral notice and the adjudicator making a decision, it is not possible to state definitely what the other elements of an adjudication may be. The following are typical examples. These may individually be required by the adjudicator, or a combination of them may be used.

Written questions

The adjudicator may provide written questions for answer by the parties. This will arise where the adjudicator having given initial consideration to the matters referred is left with specific queries.

Meetings

A meeting may be called by the adjudicator. Such meetings can take many forms and can be of varying formality, essentially depending upon the wishes of the adjudicator. Some adjudicators in a final account type dispute will take a very informal approach, going through large numbers of items of the account with the key witness from each party and generally making his decision on each at the time on an item-by-item basis. Other meetings may be more formal, with each party represented by a solicitor or barrister and the process is conducted more formally – with proof of witness statements and cross-examination taking place as if in arbitration. A meeting may be on site and the adjudicator may wish to see some of the work carried out.

There are two key things to ensure if advising a party as to a meeting. First, the adjudicator should be persuaded to produce an agenda for the meeting. Alternatively, an agenda should be proposed. Experience tells that meetings are an expensive element of the whole adjudication process and the time spent should therefore be focused on the important issues in dispute. Without an agenda the meetings can become something of a 'free-for-all' and less is achieved. Second, preparation should be made to ensure that a party is ready with all the points that are to be made to the adjudicator. The party should, of course, also ensure that all these points are then conveyed to the adjudicator at the meeting.

Further submissions

Further submissions may be provided by each party. This is a very frequent occurrence where a referring party, on receipt of the response, will seek to produce a reply. The responding party may then wish to produce a further response, and so on. As far as an adjudicator is concerned, further rounds of submissions will become progressively less useful, but against this an advisor to a party will want to ensure that important points are not missed. If important points do arise a party should not wait to be directed to produce a reply by the adjudicator but should simply draw it up and submit it. It will be very unusual for an adjudicator wholly to ignore a submission from a party.

The decision

The effect of the decision is prescribed by the Construction Act, as described above. Mistakes of law and of fact will not invalidate the decision and there is no direct appeal available. The decision is binding on the parties, but only temporarily so. The whole matter is open for subsequent litigation or arbitration or, indeed, disposal by agreement.

If a decision is one which concerns money the effect is usually to create a debt from one party to the other. In other cases the decision may impact upon the continuing contractual relationship between the parties. For example, the dispute referred may concern how a particular valuation clause is to be construed. The decision will take effect every time that clause is subsequently utilised.

The decision is also binding on any future adjudications. It is not possible to adjudicate the same point again and subsequent adjudicators are bound by the decisions arising from previous adjudications, as well as judgments or arbitral awards.

Enforcement

The last topic in this chapter concerns what a successful party may do with an adjudication decision where the losing party fails to comply with the decision, and conversely how a losing party may resist having to comply with an adjudication decision.

As stated above there is no appeal to an arbitrator's decision and the usual approach of the court is to enforce any decision robustly, irrespective of any errors in the decision. Enforcement can only be secured through the court. In order to access the court the successful party will invariably need to instruct a solicitor and/or a barrister (in many cases barristers can now be instructed directly without an intermediary solicitor – see the section 'Direct access schemes' in Chapter 3).

The usual process is for a claim form and particulars of claim to be drafted and filed at court and served on the losing party, known as the defendant/respondent in the legal proceedings. Normally the defendant would have 14 days within which to acknowledge the claim and a further 14 days within which to supply a defence. This is clearly inimical to the purposes of adjudication under the Construction Act and the courts therefore invariably grant abridgement of the time for acknowledgement to just a few days where applied for. Once the defendant has acknowledged the claim the claimant lodges a summary judgment application. This consists of submitting a completed standard application form, a witness statement (usually by the solicitor) with appendices usually including the contract, adjudication submissions and decision. A hearing is then provided for on short notice and the court hears what the parties have to say before giving judgment. A barrister is usually the appropriate person to conduct a hearing for a party.

Usually the court will enforce the decision. However, there are a range of possible outcomes, including that the decision is partially enforced, judgment is entered but a stay on enforcement is made, or the claim may even be taken forward to a trial or dismissed. If enforced, the debt becomes a judgment debt and, where necessary, charges can be put on property, bank accounts frozen etc., until monies are paid. A solicitor is best placed to advise on these matters.

There are only a limited number of grounds upon which a defendant can resist the enforcement of an adjudication decision. Some of the typical and potentially valid points that may be raised include the following:

- The commercial relationship between the parties does not constitute a construction contract as understood under the Construction Act. The adjudication provisions in the Construction Act and Scheme therefore do not apply and the adjudicator and the decision are without jurisdiction. This may be for various reasons, for example the subject matter of the work falls within the excluded categories of work, the contract is not sufficiently in writing or one party is a residential occupier.
- There was no pre-existing dispute between the parties. If there was no pre-existing dispute there was nothing to refer for decision by an adjudicator. The decision made is therefore invalid. Putting it another way, before adjudication proceedings are commenced a dispute must have crystallised between the parties and it must be that dispute which is referred to the adjudicator and not a different dispute (see Chapter 3). This ground typically arises following poorly prepared 'ambush' adjudications. To avoid this ground it is always better for a referring party to put to the prospective responding party all the substantial facts and matters, including key documents, and to give that party an opportunity expressly to reject the claim made before any adjudication proceedings are issued.
- There is a breach of the requirement of impartiality or breach of natural justice by the adjudicator, tainting the decision made. The scope for the application of natural justice is limited by the rough-and-ready nature of the adjudication process and, particularly, the time limitations provided for. Valid grounds might include, for example, where the adjudicator had communication with one party from which the other party was excluded (*Discain Project Services* v. *Opecprime Development* [2000] BLR 402).

Enforcement is a technical legal area where the right advice from a legal professional will be necessary.

7. Mediation

Robert Evans

What is mediation?

A convenient definition is that mediation is a process conducted by an independent third party, in a strictly confidential manner, where the objective is to facilitate the parties resolving their dispute.

In order to understand properly the mediation process, it is essential to appreciate fully that the role of the mediator is not to broker a settlement between the parties, but to *assist* those parties in *negotiating* their own settlement of the dispute. Thus, the parties '*own*' the dispute and the settlement of it: they, and they alone, must decide whether to settle, and on what terms. It is therefore essential that those representing the parties at a mediation have authority to reach a settlement of the dispute, or at the very least that lines of communication are in place so that those with authority can be contacted.

One important difference between mediation and the more formal dispute resolution processes, such as litigation, arbitration or adjudication (see Chapters 4, 5 and 6) is that the parties retain control over the dispute and its settlement. Once the more formal dispute resolution processes are commenced, the proceedings will continue along recognised procedural routes and will be subject to a timetable fixed by the tribunal. Thus, the parties have no control over events and often find themselves uncontrollably proceeding along the route to a final hearing or trial and decision. All of this should be contrasted with mediation, where the parties are in complete control over the proceedings and indeed whether to continue to take part in them at all. The parties are free to decide whether to withdraw from the mediation process and whether to settle or not. It is this control of the process that empowers the parties, and leaves them with ownership of the dispute and its resolution.

That said, of course the mediator plays a central role in assisting the parties to the mediation in reaching a settlement. Mediators are invariably well trained, not just in negotiation techniques but also in techniques to break deadlock within the negotiation process between the parties. These are considered further below.

Another essential feature of the mediation process is its confidentiality. In fact, mediation is confidential on two levels. First, the whole mediation process itself is private and confidential. Only the parties and their advisors need be aware of the fact of the mediation and any settlement reached at it. In addition, negotiations and communications within the mediation are without prejudice and will generally be inadmissible in any legal, arbitral or other proceedings.

Second, and perhaps more important, everything said to the mediator in private meetings is also confidential. The mediator ought not to repeat it to the other party without express permission to do so. The purpose of this requirement is probably obvious. It enables the mediator and a party to discuss options, and that party's real needs, in confidence, knowing that the discussion will not be passed on to the other party.

The mediation is also entirely without prejudice and non-binding unless, or until, a settlement agreement between the parties is signed.

Importantly, the mediator is, and must always be (and be seen by both parties to be), neutral and independent of the parties and with no interest in the outcome of the dispute. The mediator does not take sides, and has no real interest in the terms of settlement of the dispute or whether one party might or might not consider itself to be a winner or a loser. The mediator's interest is in bringing the parties to a settlement that is acceptable to them both. (Generally references are to two-party adjudications, but there is no reason why mediations should not involve three or more parties, and in practice multi-party mediations are relatively common.)

Implicit in this is the fact that the mediator does not act as an arbitrator, judge, adjudicator or expert. The mediator's role is not to decide the dispute, or the parties' respective rights and obligations, and to impose a decision on the parties, but to assist the parties in achieving their own negotiated agreement. As set out above, the parties own the dispute and the settlement of it, and it is entirely a matter for the parties to decide whether to settle, and if so on what terms.

Why mediation works

Perhaps the most important, and obvious, reason why mediation works is that it brings the parties together and gives them an opportunity, which might not otherwise arise, to settle their dispute.

Importantly, a mediation enables senior management to hear the strengths, and perhaps more importantly the weaknesses, of the parties' cases. Often those in the decision-making capacity would only have been briefed by their own personnel or advisors, whose views of the dispute may be less than impartial, and perhaps self serving, and the mediation day itself may be the first opportunity to hear both sides of the argument.

Of course, in the mediation, the parties are brought together with the mediator. The mediator's presence is likely to be instrumental in the settlement process in that, being a neutral, an independent view is brought to the negotiations. In addition, the mediator will seek to identify the real issues separating the parties, and concentrate on those issues rather than the parties' own (often incorrectly) perceived differences. The mediator will act as a conduit for communication between the parties and their representatives and can help the parties to understand each other's cases, and explore their strengths and weaknesses, so that the parties can more readily assess their own cases realistically.

In particular, the mediator will spend much of the mediation exploring the parties' real needs and interests as opposed to their publicly stated positions. This is often crucial since stumbling blocks to settlement can be overcome by recognising and respecting the real needs of the parties, which rarely coincide with their stated positions.

It is possible to add value to a settlement. For example, in a continuing commercial relationship settlement can involve future work, or opportunities for future work. Alternatively one party can perhaps, as part of the settlement agreement, provide either free of charge or at an agreed cost additional goods or services. This is something that is simply unavailable in the more formal dispute resolution proceedings.

The mediator will be able to explore with the parties (normally separately) the alternatives to settling their dispute. Here, the mediator can investigate the best, and worst, possible outcomes to the dispute, and by this illustrate the benefits, both financial and emotional, of achieving a settlement. The mediator can reality test, causing the parties and their advisors to re-evaluate the risks involved in proceeding with the dispute.

Central to the success of the mediation is the role of the mediator. It is essential that the mediator establishes the trust and confidence of the parties to the mediation from the outset so that they can discuss openly and frankly their thoughts on the dispute and the mediation. The key to this, of course, is the mediator's duty of confidentiality in the mediation. As will be considered later in this chapter, a substantial part of the mediation itself will be taken up by the mediator 'exploring' the parties' interests, emotions, strengths and weaknesses. Armed with this information, the mediator is well placed to understand and overcome the parties' emotions, and any emotional blockages that may be preventing the parties from negotiating a settlement. It is surprising how often, in practice, one party to the dispute may put at the forefront of its deliberations, and indeed the basis for settlement, something that the other party regards as quite unimportant. Thus, the mediator will both be able to assist the parties in understanding each other's case and be able to assist each party to better understand its own case.

Mediations will often commence once the informal process of negotiation has reached deadlock. Here again, the mediator's unique position makes it possible to overcome the deadlock, allowing the parties to save face by moving from what might have been publicly expressed intransigent positions. The mediator can suggest new avenues to explore, perhaps involving 'adding value', or can break the problem down into discrete elements, each of which can be focused on independently and without regard to the apparent deadlock.

Finally, the mediation will focus the parties' minds on settlement and looking to the future, rather than re-examining the past.

Facilitative and evaluative approaches

A facilitative approach to mediation is one in which the mediator does not give opinions, or pass judgment, on the parties' respective positions or cases, but seeks to bring the parties together for a commercial resolution of their dispute which meets the parties' real needs. This is done without considering or adjudicating upon the underlying rights and liabilities of the parties in any detail.

In contrast, evaluative mediation will permit the parties to investigate through the mediator the respective rights and liabilities of the parties, and the mediator may be asked to give an opinion on the merits of the dispute, or a part of it.

It would be wrong to consider facilitative and evaluative mediation as two mutually exclusive alternatives. In reality, a mediator is likely to adopt an approach that falls somewhere between the two, and whether this falls closer to the evaluative or to the facilitative approach will largely depend on the style or approach of the mediator, the attitude of the parties or their advisors, and their own perceptions of the merits of their cases. It is quite possible that the mediation will involve elements of both approaches. Ultimately, it is for the mediator to assess which is likely to be most effective for any particular dispute and for the parties to it.

However, there are dangers in the mediator expressing an opinion as to the merits of the dispute. On the one hand, a party may be disappointed at the mediator's expressed perception of the merits, and may feel that the mediator is taking sides against that party. That party may also lose trust or confidence in the mediator, and once this happens it is difficult for the mediator to re-establish it and to communicate effectively. On the other hand, a positive opinion from the mediator on a party's case may cause it to harden its position within the negotiations, which may make achieving a settlement more difficult.

Whichever approach is followed, the mediator should avoid losing his or her neutrality and impartiality. As noted in the definition of mediation set out above, one of the essential elements of mediation is the independence of the mediator. By expressing any opinions as to the strict legal rights and liabilities of the parties, there may be an appearance of loss of neutrality and independence. No doubt a mediator will have worked hard with the parties both before and during the mediation to win their trust and confidence, but trust and confidence are commodities that are easily lost, and once lost will be even harder to regain.

One of the strengths of mediation as a dispute resolution process is its flexibility and a skilled mediator will adapt his or her style and approach to the mediation to meet the circumstances in each case. Thus, if the mediation is running into difficulty, then the mediator can modify his or her approach to suit.

When to use mediation

As appears from the definition above, the pre-requisite for mediation is a dispute between the parties. Other than the existence of the dispute, there are, and can be, no hard-and-fast rules as to when is the appropriate time to mediate.

In some circumstances, particularly where there is an ongoing relationship between the parties, the parties may consider it appropriate to mediate their dispute before commencing formal legal proceedings, such as arbitration or litigation, perhaps even whilst the dispute is still fresh and the parties' developing positions have yet to become entrenched. Mediation is now encouraged by the courts either prior to, or during, the litigation process, and a party may be penalised on costs if it unreasonably refuses to participate in a mediation (this is addressed more fully in Chapter 4). It can also be appropriate during the course of arbitration in the same way.

As to the timing of mediation during a more formal dispute resolution process, there are again no hard-and-fast rules. In many respects, the earlier the mediation is held the better, since costs of the litigation or arbitration will be lower and they will be less of a factor in achieving a settlement. However, one or other of the parties often wishes certain stages in the litigation or arbitration process to have passed, so that they can be better informed as to the case that is being advanced against them, and indeed as to their own case. A party may seek to mediate after the close of formal pleadings, or perhaps after the disclosure of documentation process has taken place, so that the other party's documents are available for the purposes of the mediation, or even after the service of written evidence in the form of witness statements and experts' reports. However, whilst a successful mediation at this stage will save the time and costs of trial itself, it is likely that the parties will have incurred significant costs in the litigation or arbitration process in getting to this stage and, as noted above, this may be an additional hurdle to overcome in reaching settlement.

Appointing a mediator: CEDR and other bodies

There is no formal, statutory or indeed other legal framework for mediation of engineering disputes. It is entirely consensual and depends upon the agreement of the parties, both as to their participation in the mediation and in the appointment of the appropriate mediator for the particular dispute.

Where possible, the parties, or their advisors, will seek to agree upon an experienced and suitably qualified mediator. However, there are a number of independent bodies involved in mediation, such as the Centre for Effective Dispute Resolution (CEDR – contact details are set out in Box 6.2). These bodies can assist the parties intending to attempt to resolve their dispute by mediation by nominating trained and qualified mediators and providing formal mediation agreements.

Many firms of solicitors specialising or experienced in engineering dispute resolution have experience of mediation and can provide advice as to selecting and appointing a mediator or seeking an appointment through one of the independent bodies.

In addition, the Technology and Construction Bar Association maintains a mediation panel containing Queen's Counsel and junior counsel experienced in mediation who can be appointed by agreement between the parties. Some of the specialist building and engineering barristers' chambers also provide mediation services, by which a member of those chambers is appointed mediator and rooms and other facilities can be provided at the chambers for the mediation.

A mediator will normally insist on entering into a formal multi-partite agreement with all of the parties. Each mediator, or the body that appoints or nominates the mediator, should have their own form of agreement. A sample agreement is set out in Box 7.1.

Box 7.1: Sample form of agreement for the appointment of a mediator

TERMS OF APPOINTMENT

Mr A. Barrister, Mediator

Once appointed, the Mediator's professional fees will be calculated as follows:

All preparation work will be charged on the basis of [£   ] per hour.

The Mediator's appearance at the mediation meeting or meetings will be charged at [£   ] per hour.

Any work required following the mediation will be also be charged at the rate of [£   ] per hour.

All fees billed are subject to 17.5% VAT.

The Parties will each be invoiced for 50% of the fees incurred and those fees must be settled within 28 days of billing.

The Parties will be jointly and severally responsible for the Mediator's fees.

Neither party may have access to any of the Mediator's notes or call the Mediator as a witness in any proceedings relating to the Dispute.

For the avoidance of doubt the Mediator will be acting as an independent specialist and not as an arbitrator. The Mediator, in performing his functions set out herein, is not and will not be representing or giving legal advice to or upholding or protecting (or attempting to uphold or protect) any rights of any of the parties.

The Mediator shall not be liable to any of the parties for any act or omission whatsoever in connection with the services provided by the Mediator pursuant to this appointment. For the avoidance of doubt, this exclusion extends to negligent acts and omissions.

These terms shall be governed by and construed in accordance with English law.

The mediation

Whilst the mediation day, or even days, gives opportunity to settle the dispute, it is not necessarily the start of the process (some mediations might take several days, particularly in complex disputes involving more than two parties). Preparation is important, both to the parties and the mediator, and a good mediator will invariably contact each party, or their representative, in advance with a view to discussing their position and approach to the mediation, and indicating the likely form of the mediation day. The mediator will probably also seek to establish something about the representative of each party attending the mediation itself. This initial contact will be the start of the important process by which the mediator seeks to win the trust and confidence of the parties.

As to those representatives, it is important that a representative of each of the parties with authority to settle attends, or at the very least lines of communication are in place between those attending and those with authority to settle. In many circumstances, parties will attend a mediation with their legal advisors, solicitors and sometimes counsel. Experts may attend, but in many respects it is preferred that they do not since this may result in the parties becoming unnecessarily reliant upon the detailed facts and expert opinions.

When preparing for the mediation, the mediator will probably seek to ensure that there is, where possible, a degree of parity between the parties and their representatives attending the mediation. This ensures that a party does not feel overwhelmed by the presence of large numbers of advisors or other professionals attending for the other party.

It is important that both the parties and the mediator are aware in advance of those attending for each party. In particular, the mediator will be interested to know whether the parties or their representatives have experienced mediation before and whether they are looking for a particular style or approach from the mediator.

Most mediators will request each party to prepare a short position paper setting-out its case on the dispute, and what it (at least openly) is seeking from it. Reference will probably be made to previous attempts to settle, and any current offers as between the parties.

Each position paper will usually have attached documents relative to that party's case, including, where necessary, copies of contracts, specifications, drawings and correspondence between the parties and their representatives. Depending on the timing of the mediation, it may be that the parties have instructed experts, and their reports (or drafts of them) may be made available as well.

Position papers are important documents as they give each party an opportunity to state its case, not just for the benefit of the mediator, but also to inform the decision-making representatives of the other party. It is essential that each party should be provided with a copy of the other party's position paper and documentation.

A model position statement is given in Box 7.2 at the end of this chapter.

The mediator will probably also use the initial contact with the parties to ensure that the mediation agreement is itself acceptable to the parties so that, if not signed in advance, it can be signed by the parties on the day.

As for the mediation day itself, once again there are, and can be, no hard-and-fast rules. The day itself will often be long and tiring, and one of the first priorities of the mediator is to ensure that the venue is suitable, that the parties are comfortable for the full duration of the mediation and that there are appropriate refreshments available throughout the day. It is also useful to have typing facilities available so that if an agreement is reached, it can be set down in writing and signed by the parties there and then. There must be a separate room for each of the parties to the mediation, as well as a room in which all of the parties can meet with the mediator in joint session.

The format of the day will largely depend upon the approach of the mediator to the particular dispute, but perhaps the most usual two-party mediation procedure would involve the following:

(1) The mediator personally meets and settles the parties, having a brief discussion with each as to any developments since any previous communication. The mediator should also take the opportunity to explain a little bit about the process, and the likely course of the day. Once again this is an important part of the process by which the mediator builds the trust and confidence of the parties.

(2) A joint session at which the parties are introduced (if necessary), the mediator explains the likely course of the day, and reminds the parties of the essential elements of the mediation (confidentiality, privacy, etc.). The mediator is then likely to invite the parties, one at a time, and in an order that has been carefully selected and notified to the parties in advance, to make their introductory remarks and opening statement. The opening statement is important, and the mediator will probably have requested the parties to give this their best shot, since what is said will be heard by those representing the other party. Usually, it is not sufficient merely to read the opening statement. One of the first questions the mediator may ask each of the parties when seeing them separately following the initial joint meeting is whether they have any thoughts or views on the opening statement of the other party. Often the response will be that they have heard nothing new and, if that is the case, it has been a wasted opportunity.

(3) Thereafter, it is likely that the mediator will initially meet with each party separately. These meetings may be long or short, depending on the circumstances, and there may be several rounds of them.

(4) The mediator will have the power, if appropriate, to bring the parties back into joint session at any time and will probably do so at some stage, if only at the settlement phase.

Most mediations will follow a fairly standard three-stage process, although often the parties will not be aware of the three stages or the movement from one stage to the next, which inevitably overlap at least to some extent. The stages are as follows:

(1) exploration phase
(2) bargaining phase
(3) concluding phase.

Each of these phases is considered separately in the following sub-sections.

The exploration phase

This is the opportunity for the mediator to build rapport with the parties, and to gain the confidence and trust of the parties. The mediator's role here is largely to listen to the parties, with a view to clarifying and understanding the issues and establishing what the parties' real needs and concerns behind the dispute are. Often, even in a substantial commercial dispute, there is some underlying point of principle, or perhaps personality, that must be resolved in order for the whole dispute to be resolved. The exploration phase gives the mediator the opportunity to talk one-to-one with the parties and to explore such matters so that they can be addressed during the remainder of the mediation.

It is also an important opportunity for the mediator to understand the nature and basis of any previous offers of settlement. This will ensure that the mediation, and any negotiations in it, starts at the correct place. The history of negotiations between the parties, and an analysis of the offers and counteroffers by the parties, may give some indication as to the likely basis of settlement and the probable range in which a financial settlement may occur.

It is important for the future conduct of the mediation that the exploration stage is not rushed. There may be occasions when a mediator may spend several hours with one party or the other in this phase, and this time will inevitably be time well spent. There may be a perception by the parties that the mediator is moving matters too slowly, if indeed at all, but experience suggests that rushing the exploration phase may diminish the prospects of successfully mediating the dispute.

In other circumstances, the mediation may have moved from the exploration stage to the bargaining phase only to find it necessary to return to the exploration phase to investigate a matter not previously or fully addressed.

The mediator should always be conscious of both parties throughout the exploration phase. Thus, when starting a private meeting with one of the parties, the mediator is likely to explain to the other party what is about to happen, and perhaps give a rough time estimate as to how long the meeting might last. If it is necessary for the meeting to exceed that time, the mediator should return to the other party to explain the situation, and perhaps give a further time estimate. At all stages, the mediator should inform both parties that they should not read anything into the fact that more, or less, time is being spent with one party than the other.

One of the main tools at the disposal of the mediator is reality testing. Whilst this may take place in the bargaining phase, rather than the exploration phase, the experienced mediator should use the exploration phase as an opportunity to prepare the parties for reality testing, and for the fact that settlement is likely to involve both parties moving from their stated positions.

Central to that expectation of movement are the parties' real needs, rather than their publicly stated positions. As noted above, exploring and establishing the parties' real needs is one of the principal reasons why mediation works, and why it has such a high success rate. It is during the exploration phase that the mediator will seek to establish the parties' real needs with a view to identifying (and thereafter addressing) those matters that are truly the differences between the parties.

The mediator will, however, always be conscious of maintaining the trust of both parties and the undertakings as to confidentiality are crucial to this. As noted above, the mediator should treat everything said by a party in a private meeting as confidential and should only seek to pass it on to the other party with express permission, and the parties should be sufficiently confident in the mediator to discuss the dispute and their real needs openly and frankly.

The mediator should be conscious that it is the parties that set the agenda, and not the mediator. Thus, it is inappropriate to investigate matters that the mediator considers to be important but which the parties themselves consider to be peripheral at best.

Finally, before leaving one party to meet with the other, the mediator may well ask the party to carry out some exercise, perhaps investigate documents or review one or the other party's figures. This serves not only to keep the party involved while the mediator is absent, but can often provide useful information and analysis for the bargaining phase of the mediation.

The bargaining phase

This is the part of the mediation when the possible terms upon which a settlement may be reached can be discussed in detail. This stage will (or at least should) continue until the parties have reached their agreement (or it has come to the point where it is clear that they will be unable to reach an agreement). It is inevitable that during this phase a sticking point will be reached, and here the skilful mediator is essential. The key job will be to break the apparent deadlock, and to do so the mediator will have to negotiate skilfully and use techniques such as reality testing.

It is during this phase of the mediation that time spent in the exploration phase will start to pay dividends. For example, the mediator will have explored the parties' real needs and ascertained any potential emotional blockages. Armed with this information, the mediator will be able to identify what is important to one party and what is important to the other. Thus, the mediator may suggest ways of increasing the attractiveness of an offer, without increasing the cost. For example, it might have become apparent that a particular item of claim is one upon which one party feels very strongly, and that that party might be prepared to accept a lesser overall offer provided the particular item of claim was recognised in full. The mediator can suggest to the offeree that the offer should be structured in a way to achieve this.

It must be recognised that this phase can, and probably will, reach apparent deadlock. There can be many reasons for this, and experience shows that most mediations reach a point such as this at some stage. Once again, the experienced mediator will be skilled at dealing with apparent deadlock and will seek to identify the cause of it and investigate ways to overcome it.

The mediator will seek to break the deadlock using a number of techniques. Perhaps the simplest technique is to ask the parties what they would like the mediator to do. Given that the alternative to reopening the negotiations is likely to be a failure to reach a settlement, this in practice is a powerful tool to break the deadlock. It can, and normally would, be combined with a further reality test so that the parties can fully appreciate and understand the risks they face if they do not achieve a negotiated settlement during the course of the mediation.

During the bargaining phase the mediator can, if it seems to be appropriate, continue to meet with each party on its own, discussing offers and taking counterproposals back and forth, or the mediator can, and in many circumstances will, bring the parties together so that fine detail can be discussed directly between the relevant representatives from the parties. However, the mediator should always be mindful of personalities and the possibility that such a meeting might be counterproductive. The mediator should also consider whether to suggest bringing both parties' complete teams, including advisors, together, or whether it should be a meeting between the two principal decision-makers without legal or other advisors.

Throughout all of this the mediator and the parties must recognise that it is the parties that own the problem and its solution, and that the settlement rests in their hands. It is not for the mediator to press the parties for a particular solution in order to break the deadlock. It is always to be left to the parties, albeit with the assistance of the mediator, to achieve their own settlement.

During this phase, it is important that the parties and the mediator fully understand the offers that are being made, and that the offers are complete and deal with all the matters in dispute. It is not uncommon for broad offers to be exchanged and for agreement to be reached on them only for one party to raise some further outstanding matter (for example, copyright on drawings, or even VAT or interest and costs). If this happens it is necessary to return to the bargaining phase so that the parties can once again reach a complete and comprehensive settlement. However, these matters are best avoided, and it is important for the mediator, as well as the parties, to understand the exact nature of the offer that is being made or accepted so that there is no confusion and appearance of backtracking.

The concluding phase

The concluding phase arises when the parties have, at least in principle, reached a settlement. In the concluding phase, it is the responsibility of the parties (and not the mediator) to draft a formal settlement agreement. Often during this part of the process, further disputes over detailed matters which had not occurred to the parties during the detailed bargaining phase will arise, often including matters such as VAT or VAT invoicing, costs and the like. These matters will need to be resolved in the same way as the principal dispute and using the same techniques, and often necessitate a return to the bargaining phase.

It is important that the settlement agreement is sufficiently well drafted that it is legally binding on the parties and enforceable should any dispute arise on it. In addition, it is important that it deals fully with the dispute between the parties and the basis upon which they settle, and its terms are clear and certain, so that further disputes as to the meaning and effect of the settlement agreement can be avoided. Often the parties will rely upon professional advisors for this part of the mediation process. It should be noted that the mediator will not normally be involved in the detailed drafting of the agreement. However, the mediator will consider it and may raise questions as to potential areas of ambiguity and uncertainty.

The mediator, and indeed the parties, should be careful to publicly not state views on whether the settlement is considered to be a fair or good one, as the case may be. One party may feel that it has done less well out of the mediation and the settlement resulting from it than the other, or than it might have expected, and the mediator should be sensitive to both parties' feelings.

Finally, it must be appreciated that there will be circumstances where settlement is not reached during the course of the mediation day (or days). However, a good mediator will not simply walk away from the parties and their dispute at the end of the day, but will keep in touch with the parties thereafter with a view to continuing informally the mediation process and continuing to seek to give the parties the opportunity to settle their dispute. The parties should make the best use of this further opportunity, as, in practice, it is surprising how often disputes that do not settle during the mediation itself subsequently settle, either with the further involvement of the mediator or directly between the parties and their advisors, using the mediation, and the negotiations in it, as a springboard to closing the parties' remaining differences.

Box 7.2: Model mediation position paper

IN THE MATTER OF A MEDIATION

BETWEEN:

AB CONSTRUCTION LTD

– and –

CD PROPERTIES LTD

POSITION STATEMENT OF
AB CONSTRUCTION LTD

Introduction

1. This Mediation arises out of a contract (hereinafter 'the Contract') made on the ICE Conditions of Contract, 7th Edition, Measurement Version between AB Construction Ltd (hereinafter 'ABC'), as Contractor, and CD Properties Ltd (hereinafter 'CDP'), as Employer, whereby CDP engaged ABC to construct and complete certain works (hereinafter 'the Works'), namely the enabling works comprising drainage and sewerage works, and construction of roads, for a housing development at Thames Gateway.
2. The Contract was made on 1st January 2005, and the time for completion of the Works was 30th June 2005. In fact, for the reasons set out below, ABC were not certified as having substantially completed the Works until some 6 weeks later, namely 15th August 2005.
3. It is ABC's case that it is entitled to an extension of time of 6 weeks by reason of unforeseen ground conditions encountered during the installation of the drainage and the late provision of information by the Engineer.
4. In addition, ABC claims the cost incurred by reason of the ground conditions and late provision of information.
5. CDP, on the other hand denies that the ground conditions were reasonably unforeseeable, and also denies that the Engineer provided information late.
6. Thus, in summary, the dispute concerns:

   (i) ABC's entitlement to an extension of time of 6 weeks.

(ii) ABC's entitlement to cost of some £100,000 either under the Contract, or as damages for breach of contract, by reason of the ground conditions and/or the late provision of information by the Engineer.

7. The total value of ABC's claims is some £100,000. In addition, CDP has intimated that it proposes to deduct liquidated damages for the 6 weeks delay totalling some £60,000.

8. Each of the elements of the dispute is considered separately, and briefly, below.

THE EXTENSION OF TIME CLAIM

Ground Conditions

9. This claim arises out of Clause 12 of the Conditions of Contract, and it is ABC's case that it encountered physical conditions which could not reasonably have been foreseen by an experienced Contractor comprising groundwater level some 2 m higher than ABC anticipated from the site investigation provided at tender. Accordingly, ABC gave notice by letter dated 1st February 2005 of the ground conditions, and sought instructions from the Engineer. In the event, the Engineer decided that the conditions were reasonably foreseeable, and rejected the claim, and issued no instructions. Accordingly, ABC carried out the Works including installing drainage in and below the groundwater table, using dewatering equipment as necessary.

10. As a result of the physical conditions, ABC incurred additional costs in bringing to the site and utilising dewatering equipment, and suffered a delay of some 6 weeks to the drainage works. Accordingly, ABC is entitled to, and claims, a 6 week extension of time for completion of the Works, together with the additional cost (and profit thereon) pursuant to Clause 12(6) of the Conditions of Contract.

11. By reason of the extension of time, CDP has no entitlement to deduct liquidated damages for delay.

Late Information

12. In addition, the Engineer was required to provide to CDP detailed setting-out and alignment information for the roadworks. Although ABC's Clause 14 Programme indicated that earthworks for roadwork would commence on 1st March 2005, it was not until 30th March 2005 that the Engineer provided this information.

13. This delay in the provision of the setting-out information caused a further 1 month concurrent delay with the delay to the drainage works, and resulted in ABC incurring additional costs, including costs of additional earthworks and roadworks labour and plant. A full breakdown of these costs appears at Appendix 1 hereto.

CDP's Defences

14. In the course of correspondence between the Engineer and CDP itself, CDP has sought to deny ABC's claims on the basis that:
    (i) The groundwater table did not amount to physical conditions and/or that it should in any event reasonably have been foreseen by an experienced Contractor.
    (ii) The absence of any request from ABC for the roadwork setting-out information; and
    (iii) In respect of all claims, the absence of any notice pursuant to Clause 53 of the Conditions of Contract.

15. ABC contends that these contentions are misconceived, in fact and in law, and relies upon the following:
    (i) The groundwater clearly amounts to physical conditions. The site investigation information provided with the tender documents and upon which ABC's tender was based clearly showed the water table at, or below, the maximum depth of drainage and sewerage excavation.
    (ii) Whilst it is right that no specific request was made for the setting-out information, this is not fatal to ABC's claim, since the date upon which earthworks were due to commence was clearly stated in the (approved) Clause 14 Programme; and
    (iii) Even if notices were not provided by ABC pursuant to Clause 53, by Clause 53(5), the giving of sufficient notice is not a condition precedent to the validity of the claim. The Engineer has not been prejudiced by the absence of notice.

Summary

16. By way of summary, ABC is entitled to an extension of time (and therefore it is not liable for liquidated damages) together with a total sum of £100,000 plus VAT and interest. At the date of this Mediation, ABC has indicated that it would be willing to accept a sum of £75,000 (with no liability for liquidated damages) in full and final settlement of its claims. On the other hand, CDP has offered to settle this matter on the basis of a payment to ABC of £15,000 (allowing for ABC's liability for liquidated damages). This is not acceptable to ABC.

17. Both parties have agreed to participate in this Mediation, and have agreed to the appointment of the Mediator. For its part, ABC makes it clear that it comes to the Mediation with an open mind and the firm intention to have this dispute successfully mediated. ABC recognises the value of achieving a settlement, not just for the immediate dispute, but also in recognition of the ongoing commercial relationship between the parties.

18. That said, however, ABC is confident in its position that it is entitled to substantial sums in respect of the clear breach of contract in supplying late. In addition, ABC can have no liability to CDP for liquidated damages.

Attachments

19. A copy of the Conditions of Contract, the tender site investigation and relevant correspondence, instructions and valuations are attached to the Position Statement.

8. Expert determination

Jonathan Lee

Introduction

The alternative dispute resolution processes of expert determination provides the parties to a dispute with unique opportunities. In essence the term 'expert determination' describes a process by which the parties agree that a third party, who is of a relevant discipline (the 'expert') and is independent of both parties, is to be engaged to answer a particular question or determine a particular dispute, and that both parties are to be bound by that expert's decision. The process can, therefore, result in a fast, binding and final resolution of the issues referred to the expert.

Expert determination is also flexible. It is based entirely upon an agreement between the parties and so the parties have the opportunity, subject to their mutual agreement, to control and tailor the process to suit their particular circumstances. For example, the parties may wish to agree, either at the time that a dispute arises or, more commonly, in advance by incorporating appropriate terms into a contract between them:

(1) who to appoint as the expert or how the expert is to be selected and appointed
(2) the question or questions that the expert is to be asked to determine
(3) the process the expert is to follow
(4) the period in which the expert is to determine the questions referred
(5) the finality of the decision, and
(6) the parties' liability for the expert's fees and the parties' costs.

Note that the term 'expert determination' is generally used to describe a process that results in a final and binding decision from an expert. However, this is not always the case – it is open to the parties to decide otherwise or to use the process to resolve disputes on an interim basis during a project. For example, in *Rhodia Chirex Ltd* v. *Laker Vent Engineering Ltd* CA [2004] BLR 75, an expert was appointed under the IChemE model form of contract to resolve a dispute over the proper value of a provisional termination certificate. The expert's decision was held by the Court of Appeal to be final and binding in respect of that provisional certificate. However, the contract also provided for a final termination certificate to be issued, so the expert's decision in this case could at some later date have become irrelevant.

The flexibility of expert determination allows it to be used in a broad array of circumstances, sometime to avoid lengthy and complex disputes from arising and at other times to resolve disputes quickly and cheaply. It is not uncommon for parties to agree that the whole process shall be concluded in a matter of days after an expert has been appointed.

Subject to the agreement of the parties, the expert is free to use his or her own knowledge, expertise and experience to investigate the issue that has been referred for determination. This is often considered to be one of the greatest strengths of expert determination. In many situations, particularly when the nature of the issue to be decided is technical, the expert will have been carefully selected to do precisely that. The expert is appointed not just to hear the parties' various contentions and to select between them, but rather to investigate the circumstances and to apply specialist knowledge and expertise in order to decide for the parties the answer to the question they have referred for determination.

Obviously, the perceived benefits of expert determination carry with them associated risks. The benefit of finality has to be weighed carefully against the consequent risk of being unable to appeal or, subject to only few exceptions, to challenge the expert's decision. The benefit of agreeing to a fast dispute resolution process has to be balanced against the risk of the procedure not allowing the depth of investigation that other procedures might have allowed.

As with all forms of dispute resolution, it is a matter of 'horses for courses'. However, when used in appropriate circumstances expert determination can provide what many engineers long for: a fast and final decision from an independent engineer whose discipline, expertise and experience make him or her ideally suited to deciding the issue that has arisen between the parties.

In many of the oldest cases dealt with by expert determination the expert was used to provide parties with a binding third-party valuation for the subject matter of their contract. This is still common, although more recently the traditional subject matters of such valuations (shares in private companies and property and rents) have expanded across the spectrum of modern commercial activities. Examples include:

- fixing the value of computer equipment
- adjusting the price of vessels or equipment depending on their actual condition
- resolving the sums to be paid under engineering contracts in respect of variations or on termination
- deciding whether goods or equipment are of the quality required by a contract
- deciding whether remedial work was required to engineering works
- deciding in respect of a performance bond whether the employer was entitled to call on the bond by reason of a breach by the contractor of its contract with the employer
- decisions over compensation for oil pollution.

In addition, and as familiarity and confidence with the effectiveness and efficiency of expert determination has become more widespread, it is becoming more common for parties to agree that any dispute arising out of a contract between them shall be, or may be, referred to an expert for a binding decision (for example, *Thames Valley Power Ltd* v. *Total Power & Gas Ltd* [2005] EWHC 2208 (Comm)). The risk to the parties in making such an agreement does appear to be high, and this would be particularly so in the context of a contract for a complex engineering project. One expert may simply not have a sufficiently broad field of expertise to cover the range of possible issues that could arise from the contract. Expert determination is more likely to be regarded as appropriate where the contract identifies particular questions or subject areas that can be matched to the known field of expertise of the proposed expert.

Expert determination versus other dispute resolution processes

The most significant feature that distinguishes expert determination from mediation, early neutral evaluation and adjudication is that it will provide the parties with a final and binding decision. Mediation and early neutral evaluation can provide circumstances in which the parties might successfully negotiate a binding agreement, but such an agreement is not always possible. Adjudication is usually conducted on the basis that the decision will be final and binding unless or until it is overturned by litigation or arbitration. It is therefore envisaged that following adjudication, the decision may only have a temporary effect and that the same issue that was referred to the adjudicator may be decided afresh. By contrast, expert determination will, because that is what the parties agree, result in a decision that is final and binding. There can be no appeal and no rehearing.

Litigation and arbitration can also provide final and binding outcomes, although they are both distinct from expert determination. Most arbitrations are accurately described as 'litigation in the private sector' (per Sir John Donaldson MR in *Northern RHA* v. *Derek Crouch* [1984] QB 644 at 670); however, the boundaries between expert determination and arbitration can appear somewhat blurred. Circumstances in which parties have agreed to expert determination have expanded from the answering of questions so as to avoid disputes from arising to include the resolution of any disputes arising out of a contract. At the same time, the Arbitration Act 1996 makes provision for arbitrators to take the initiative in ascertaining the facts and law, thereby allowing an inquisitorial element to be introduced to the traditionally adversarial nature of arbitrations. It remains the case, however, that the two processes are said to be quite distinct. This has recently been described by Cooke J in *Bernard Schulte GMBH & Co. KG and others* v. *Nile Holdings Ltd* [2004] 2 Lloyd's Rep. 352 at paragraph 95 in the following terms:

> There is an essential distinction between judicial decisions and expert decisions, although the reason for the distinction has been variously expressed. There is no useful purpose in phraseology such as 'quasi judicial' or 'quasi arbitral' as Lord Simon made plain in *Arenson* and although the use of the word 'expert' is not conclusive, the historic phrase 'acting as an expert and not as an arbitrator' connotes

a concept which is clear in its effect. A person sitting in a judicial capacity decides matters on the basis of submissions and evidence put before him, whereas the expert, subject to the express provisions of his remit, is entitled to carry out his own investigations, form his own opinion and come to his own conclusion regardless of any submissions or evidence adduced by the parties themselves. Although, contrary to what is said in some of the authorities, there are many expert determinations of matters where disputes have already arisen between the parties, there is a difference in the nature of the decision made and as Kendall points out in paragraphs 1.2, 15.6.1 and 16.9.1 the distinction is drawn and the effect spelt out, namely that there is no requirement for the rules of natural justice or due process to be followed in an expert determination in order for that determination to be valid and binding between the parties.

The reference to 'Kendall' here being to the book *Expert Determination* by John Kendall (published by Sweet & Maxwell), which has been cited with approval in numerous cases and which is now in its third edition (2001).

This passage emphasises two distinguishing characteristics. First is that experts are engaged to employ their skills and expertise to conduct their own investigations in order to answer the questions referred to them, taking such account of the submissions of the parties and the evidence that they put forward as they see fit, whereas judges and arbitrators are required to decide on the basis of the submissions and evidence. The second is that although experts must be fair and impartial, they are not bound to observe due process nor to comply with the rules of natural justice.

By way of example, since an expert is not acting in a judicial capacity the requirement that the expert is impartial is more limited in scope than when applied to judges and arbitrators. An expert's decision will be set aside if actual bias is proved since the expert would have failed to hold the balance fairly between the parties; however, in *Macro & Others* v. *Thompson & Others (No. 3)* [1997] 2 BCLC 36 (cited with approval in *Bernard Schulte GMBH & Co. KG and Others* v. *Nile Holdings Ltd*) (see reference below), Walker J decided that apparent partiality was not sufficient to set aside the decision of an expert, since this might unduly inhibit an expert with a longstanding relationship with a client in continuing to discharge his professional duty to the client.

At a practical level the following distinctions between litigation, arbitration and expert determination are of note.

Procedure

Unlike litigation and many arbitrations, where the process is usually lengthy and formal, expert determination is usually swift and relatively free of complex procedures. The parties have a free hand in deciding the procedure that is to be followed and, if none is specified, then the appointed expert is free (within the bounds of fairness and actual impartiality) to reach a decision following whatever procedure he or she sees fit. However, parties do commonly agree a basic procedural framework for expert determinations, by which each party is given an opportunity to provide the expert with relevant documents and submissions. The expert is then free to supplement that procedure (see *Bernard Schulte GMBH & Co. KG and Others* v. *Nile Holdings Ltd* [2004] 2 Lloyd's Rep. 352 at paragraph 88).

While it is in the parties' interests to establish a procedure to provide them with adequate opportunity to set out their positions to the expert, it should be remembered that the parties have usually selected expert determination in order to obtain a swift and inexpensive decision (often within a matter of a few days or weeks) and they have engaged the expert to inquire into the matter and use his or her own skill and judgment, not merely to adjudicate between the stances of the two parties.

In both arbitration and litigation concerning engineering and construction projects, it is common for each party to instruct one or more expert witnesses to express their opinions to the court or tribunal. In an expert determination, where the appointed expert has been engaged to answer a particular question by coming to his or her own decision on the point in issue, it would be unusual for the parties to instruct further experts to prepare reports as independent witnesses.

Under the Arbitration Act 1996 the courts have numerous powers to assist in the fair resolution of a dispute referred to an arbitrator. These include the appointment of an arbitrator should the parties' agreed appointment procedure fail, and the making of orders concerning, for example, the attendance of witnesses and the preservation of evidence. No such support is available in the case of an expert determination because the Arbitration Act 1996 does not apply. In the context of expert determination the court may assist in so far as difficulties are caused by a breach by one party of an implied duty to cooperate so that the expert determination can be carried out properly (see *Sudbrook Trading Estates Ltd* v. *Eggleston and Others* [1983] AC 444, and *Smith* v. *Peters* (1875) LR 20 Eq. 511, in which the court ordered one party to grant access to premises so that the expert (a valuer) could conduct his investigation by inspecting the articles he had to value). However, compared with the powers of the court in respect of arbitrations, the assistance available in respect of an expert determination is very limited and parties are therefore well advised to include adequate procedural provisions in their agreement.

International agreements

Specific legal advice should be sought if it is proposed that expert determination be used as a dispute resolution procedure for international contracts. The enforceability of the parties' agreement to be bound by the decision of an expert may depend upon the law which is applicable to the contract, the public policy of the states concerned and the legal procedures of the country in which enforcement is attempted.

The UK is a signatory to the Brussels Convention, the Lugano Convention and the New York Convention, such that the decision of judges and arbitrators carry with them the benefit of wide international enforceability without the parties having to address the underlying merits of the dispute again. However, this is not the case in respect of expert determination. In some cases it may be possible to obtain a judgment from an English court (or even an arbitration award) giving effect to an expert's decision. Reliance could then be placed upon the judgment or award when seeking to rely upon the relevant convention during any international enforcement.

Identifying the question that is to be answered

Whether the question to be answered by the expert is identified before the parties enter a contract, or whether the question to be answered or the matter to be decided arises only after a contract has been entered, it is of utmost importance that the scope of potential references and the terms of any actual reference to the expert are clear.

The issues and question that the parties agree may be referred to an expert must be defined with sufficient certainty for there to be a valid contract between the parties and between the parties and the expert. Unless the particular question is narrowly defined within the words of the contract the reference to the expert must itself define the question that the expert is being asked to answer, and that question must arise from a subject area in relation to which the parties have agreed to use expert determination.

On a practical level, ensuring that there is clarity is, of course, also prudent because the decision of the appointed expert will be final and binding on the parties.

Lack of clarity provides a further potentially serious pitfall. The jurisdiction of the expert derives from and is limited by the agreement of the parties. If the expert misconstrues what has been asked so as to answer the wrong question then any decision may be invalid, allowing any enforcement proceedings to be defended.

The parties' agreement to refer a question to an expert

If parties agree that a particular question or dispute is to be referred to expert determination but one party ignores the agreement and starts proceedings in court, the court will usually stay that action if the other party applies, at the start of those proceedings, for the court action to be stayed so that the dispute may be referred to an expert.

In *Thames Valley Power Ltd* v. *Total Gas & Power Ltd* [2005] EWHC 2208 (Comm), the court held that it had discretion as to whether to grant a stay or not because the Arbitration Act 1996 did not apply to agreements to resolve disputes by expert determination. The court accepted that the *prima facie* position was that disputes were to be determined in the manner that the parties had agreed. However, on the particular facts of the case, where there was no dispute of fact between the parties and where the only issue between the parties was how the contract should be construed and where the construction contended for by the defendant was 'erroneous and unsustainable', it was held by the court that there was no benefit to be gained in a stay since this would merely result in delay and wasted costs.

The decision in *Thames Valley Power Ltd* v. *Total Gas & Power Ltd* should, however, be regarded as the exception rather than the rule. It is likely to be rare that the facts will lead a court to the same conclusion. A more typical case is *Edward Campbell & Others* v. *OCE (UK) Ltd* [2005] EWHC 458 (Ch). In that case the agreement concerned the sale of a majority shareholding in a printing business. The agreement included terms that required a 'completion balance sheet' to be drawn up and it was agreed that any dispute as to the accuracy of that balance sheet was to be referred to a firm of chartered accountants, who were to resolve the dispute acting as experts and not arbitrators. After the sale of shares no agreement was reached over the completion balance sheet – the purchaser's position being that the balance sheet was overstated due to prior overcharging of customers by the vendors. Several disputes arose between the parties and the vendors started proceedings in court. Among their claims was a claim for a declaration that no adjustment fell to be made to the completion balance sheet. The purchaser, OCE (UK) Ltd, counterclaimed in respect of alleged breaches by the vendors of warranties that had been given as to the truth of certain statements about the company's affairs. However, in respect of the issue over the completion balance sheet and the declaration that the vendors were seeking, the purchaser argued that the court should strike out those parts of the court proceedings because of the parties' express agreement to refer such matters to expert determination. The court considered argument from the vendors that the court should accept jurisdiction over the disputed completion balance sheet because the dispute was likely to cover the same factual material as the disputed breaches of the warranties. The court, however, rejected that argument and it held that the parties' agreement to refer disputes about the completion balance sheet was clear and that the terms of the agreement contemplated that some issues would be resolved by an expert and others by the courts. The claim for a declaration was struck out, leaving the vendors to refer the issue to an expert if they wished. The balance of the case was allowed to proceed before the court.

This case demonstrates not only the fact that the court will seek to uphold a party's right to have disputes determined by an expert if that is what the parties have previously agreed, but also that the parties can by the terms of their agreement define the boundaries between issues that they want to be decided by an expert and others where they are content for litigation or arbitration to be used if disputes require resolution by a third party.

9. Early neutral evaluation

Richard Coplin

What it is and when to use it

What is ENE?

Early neutral evaluation (ENE) is an alternative dispute resolution (ADR) technique developed in the early 1990s by district courts in the United States. The original objective of ENE was to reduce the costs of the litigation process. The district courts decided to offer a programme that would occur very early in the litigation process to help lawyers and clients get an early grip on case development planning and case management.

The process was intended to give perspective to a case already being litigated, to sharpen it, and to focus not on settlement but on improving the quality of thinking of both the client and the lawyers. ENE, however, did help settle many cases. It was so successful that the process, whilst still a valuable settlement tool for use when litigation has commenced, has now also moved outside litigation and has become an ADR technique in its own right.

As its name indicates, ENE has at its heart three defining components:

(1) early – in that it is intended that the process is embarked upon before a formal litigation or arbitration process has started or right at the start of such process

(2) neutral – not surprisingly, the process is presided over by someone unconnected with the dispute or either party (the evaluator), and

(3) evaluation – in that the evaluator produces an evaluation or recommendation as to what he or she thinks is to be the likely outcome should the dispute proceed.

ENE is different from mediation in that the focus is on the evidence and the law. ENE is explicitly evaluative. In classic mediation, the mediator is not explicitly evaluative and evaluation is not a principal objective of the process. In mediation, evaluation often is indirect and could be based on information learned in confidence. In ENE, evaluation is direct and explicit, and should be based only on information that all parties know the evaluator knows. The principal purpose of mediation is settlement. ENE has multiple purposes, only one of which is settlement.

ENE is different from expert determination in that it is generally a voluntary process conducted on a confidential and without prejudice basis.

Key features of ENE

ENE is a voluntary procedure, the evaluator's recommendation (the 'evaluation') is non-binding and the process, including the submissions to the evaluator and the evaluation, are confidential.

The success of ENE lies within its ability to help define the legal and factual disputes and identify both the risks and likely outcome before vast sums of costs are spent chasing a dispute. Due to its non-binding effect, ENE is ideally suited to forming part of an overall settlement strategy. An evaluator can not only address single issues of fact or law from within a dispute, but he or she may also be asked to recommend a settlement value.

An attractive aspect of ENE is that it does not have the preconceptions sometimes associated with mediations, namely that a suggestion of mediation might appear to be an admission of weakness or a willingness to split the difference. A proposal for ENE indicates confidence in the case because of the willingness to subject it to third-party scrutiny.

What does ENE hope to achieve?

The purpose of ENE is to clarify the issues in dispute and to give an indication of the likely outcome should the dispute proceed to litigation or arbitration.

ENE assists a party in identifying and clarifying the key legal and factual issues in dispute, both in respect of their own position and that of the other side. It encourages and promotes direct communication between the parties about their claims and supporting evidence. At an early stage this can quite often be the key to unlocking the dispute.

The evaluation itself provides a 'reality check' for both clients and their lawyers and advisors and, of course, it informs the decision-makers of the parties of the relative strengths and weaknesses of their positions. Quite often this process is first undertaken at the door of the court after considerable sums of money have been spent.

Where key questions can be identified, whether they make up the whole dispute or are part of a larger dispute, it is often these simple steps which help to create the right environment for a settlement.

What does an evaluator do?

An evaluator, depending on the particular ENE agreement, sets a procedure for the parties to follow, studies materials provided by the parties, performs independent research into relevant case law (or relies on his or her own expertise), considers presentations which can be written or oral and can clarify the facts and the positions of the parties through written or oral questioning.

When the evaluator has reviewed the parties' positions and the information they have provided against his or her own research he or she produces a written evaluation of the relatives strengths and weaknesses of each party's position. If asked to do so, the evaluator may provide reasons for the evaluation.

When to use ENE

ENE works best when the dispute, or part of a dispute, involves technical or factual issues that lend themselves to expert (usually legal) evaluation. It is ideal where the dispute can be put in the form of a question to which the answer is 'yes' or 'no' or by reference to defined alternatives, such as a question of construction of a contract or where there are legal issues to be resolved against a factual or technical background.

Almost all legal disputes boil down to questions such as these – the skill is in identifying the questions as early as possible in the dispute process.

Other situations where the ENE should be considered include where the top decision-makers of one or more of the parties could be better informed about the real strengths and weaknesses of their cases, or when a dispute has become polarised and the parties' positions too far apart to consider mediation. Many parties have followed ENE with a successful mediation.

Appointing an evaluator

When the parties have agreed to an ENE of their dispute, or part of it, the next steps are to agree an evaluator with the other side and to enter into an agreement, which will be between the parties to the dispute and the evaluator.

Choosing an evaluator

It is particularly important for the parties to agree on the identity of the evaluator (or panel) and to feel confident that the evaluator is sufficiently expert in the law and the subject matter of the dispute so that the resulting evaluation has the required weight and influence.

The right evaluator will depend on the nature of the dispute in question. Legal and factual disputes generally lend themselves to a legally qualified evaluator, whereas expert factual issues might be better served by an expert in the appropriate field, or where the issues cross a number of areas of expertise a panel may be necessary to give the evaluation the required weight and influence.

It is customary to suggest more than one evaluator to the other side (usually three) to avoid giving the impression that he or she has been specifically chosen for this dispute. Alternatively a party may suggest a body (which has more than one evaluator in the appropriate field on its books) to make the appointment.

The ENE agreement

In many cases, those offering ENE services will have a standard agreement which can stand as it is or be amended by the parties as they see fit. The agreement will cover things such as the procedure to be adopted, the evaluator's role in that procedure, the type of presentations that may be made (written and/or oral) and whether the evaluation will include reasons or not.

The agreement may define the procedure to be used quite precisely or it may give the evaluator a greater degree of independence in the procedure. Usually the evaluator will be given sufficient rein to enable him or her to investigate the issues thoroughly and the scope to identify, in the evaluation, any matters which may be helpful to the parties.

Often the only real decision that needs to be made is whether the ENE should involve a hearing. Where there is witness or expert evidence which is disputed this can be extremely useful, but many ENEs involve a paper-only exercise, particularly where the only real issues are legal.

Typically an agreement (which will have a hearing) will provide the following:

(1) The evaluator shall be responsible for the conduct of the ENE. A preliminary meeting will be held with the parties to discuss the conduct and procedure of the ENE and to give directions.

(2) The parties will exchange with each other and send to the evaluator copies of a paginated bundle containing:

    (i)   a concise summary of its case in the dispute

    (ii) witness statements (if relevant) to which the summary refers

    (iii) any expert reports (if relevant) to which the summary refers

    (iv) any other documents which the parties wish the evaluator to consider, and

    (v) full copies of any case law relied upon.

(3) Each party will provide to the other side and the evaluator a copy of any written response to the other party's written submission.

(4) Upon receipt of all the above, the evaluator will organise a conference between the evaluator and the parties. At the conference, each party shall make a presentation to the evaluator summarising its position and addressing any issues identified by the evaluator. The evaluator shall determine the duration of each presentation and response. The evaluator may question the parties and request further written information or evidence.

(5) The evaluator will issue the evaluation within 10 working days of the conference or such other period as may be agreed with the parties.

(6) Each party may appoint one or more representatives or legal advisors to assist, advise and/or attend.

(7) The parties undertake to each other and agree that the entire process of the ENE (including any submissions, the written evaluation and any other documents produced) is confidential and will not be disclosed without the prior written consent of the other parties.

(8) The fees and expenses of the evaluator, as well as any other expenses relating to the ENE, will be borne by the parties in equal shares.

(9) Each party will bear its own costs and expenses of its participation in the ENE.

Preparation for the evaluation

Usually, the first task will be to prepare a written evaluation statement. The statement should be a clear and logical statement of the dispute and the reasons that a particular view should be preferred. It should also identify any documents relied upon, a summary of any cases relied upon and copies of the judgments in those cases as appropriate, with a summary of witness or expert evidence as appropriate. Usually, there will be an opportunity to respond to the written evaluation statements of the other side.

The parties may already have engaged lawyers through whom the process has been co-ordinated. However, if there is an oral presentation to be made it is worth considering obtaining legal representation specifically for that presentation, particularly if the issue is one of a legal nature.

The evaluation decision/recommendation

The evaluation decision/recommendation itself may contain only a simple answer to the issues in dispute. It can, however, particularly if the parties have given the evaluator a broad jurisdiction to look at the dispute, contain helpful ideas as to the next steps that could be taken. For example, the evaluator may identify the answer to a legal question and indicate the steps that ought to be taken to evaluate the financial consequences of the recommendation. If the recommendation was the result of an exercise of judgment then the evaluation may also contain an identification of the risks to both sides of proceeding to litigation or arbitration.

The evaluation should at least form the basis for further negotiation and can of course form part of the material upon which a mediation is based. Even if a settlement is not ultimately reached, the process of focusing on the facts and the law, together with the evaluation, which should identify the key issues if the parties have not, may enable the parties to narrow the dispute and minimise the costs of litigation or arbitration.

Conclusion

ENE is a relatively recent introduction into the ADR market and, in part due to the success of other ADR processes, it has not received the profile it deserves. ENE has recently been recognised by the courts in the UK. In appropriate cases the Technology and Construction Court (TCC) now encourages its users, with the consent of all parties, to ask a TCC judge to provide an ENE, either in respect of the full case or of particular issues arising within it.

Given that it is possible to obtain an evaluation from a judge who may otherwise have been presiding over a lengthy and expensive trial, it would be surprising if the profile of ENE did not rise considerably over the coming years.

10. International dispute resolution

Dr Robert Gaitskell, QC

Introduction

Since the UK's construction industry successfully secures work world-wide, it is often involved in international construction and engineering disputes. The procedures by which such disputes are dealt with are fixed by the terms of the dispute resolution clause within the contract in question. International construction and engineering contracts invariably specify that, if other attempts at resolving a dispute have failed, the parties should resort to arbitration.

There is a powerful reason why arbitration, rather than litigation within a court system, is preferred in such circumstances. Invariably, where a UK contractor or consultant is doing work abroad, it will feel uncomfortable having a dispute about its work in that foreign country being dealt with by a local judge. Arbitration avoids this problem. For small disputes, the arbitration clause will generally permit a sole arbitrator to be appointed, either by agreement between the parties or by an independent inter-national appointing body. For larger disputes, the arbitration clause will generally provide for a three-person tribunal, where each of the disputing parties appoints one arbitrator, and the two appointees then agree a third person to act as chairperson. In this way, both sides have confidence in the impartiality of the tribunal as a whole.

For bigger projects it is becoming increasingly common for the dispute resolution clause within the contract to provide for a dispute board (DB). In essence, a DB is involved from the outset of the project, attending site about three times a year, and, if necessary, conducting serial adjudi-cations. This results in disputes being 'nipped in the bud' before they can develop into arbitrations. Nevertheless, arbitration remains as the ultimate procedure if either or both parties are dissatisfied with the DB's decisions or recommendations.

Besides arbitration and DBs, there is growing usage of mediation, adjudication and expert determination for international disputes. All of these procedures are considered in more detail in the course of this chapter. However, employing any type of dispute resolution procedure should be avoided if possible (see Chapter 2).

Choosing the dispute resolution procedure

Assuming the dispute resolution clause in the contract contains a range of options, an aggrieved party will have some choice as regards how to resolve its dispute in the quickest and most cost effective manner. This will involve considering the pros and cons of whichever procedures are catered for in the dispute resolution clause. Generally, for international disputes litigation in the courts is highly unattractive to at least one party and so need not be considered further.

The following sections in this chapter discuss how the various dispute resolution procedures can be applied to international disputes. The procedures that can be considered for use are:

- arbitration – also see Chapter 5
- adjudication/dispute board – also see Chapter 6 as to adjudication; the DB procedure is dealt with in this chapter
- mediation/early neutral evaluation – also see Chapters 7 and 9
- expert determination – also see Chapter 8.

Arbitration

Several types of procedure can be considered for use in international disputes

- procedures administered by appointing and supervising bodies: the International Chamber of Commerce (ICC), the London Court of International Arbitration (LCIA), Swiss Chambers of Commerce, etc.
- the UNCITRAL procedure (see Chapter 5), which the parties themselves administer
- ad hoc procedures.

Most international arbitrations are conducted under the supervision of one or other of the principal international appointing bodies, such as ICC, LCIA or the Swiss Chambers of Commerce – see the addresses in Box 10.1. Using the administrative support of such a body requires the parties to pay fees to that body to cover the appointment of the tribunal and the subsequent supervision of the tribunal's activities through to the final issuing of the award. The parties generally feel that the costs involved are well-spent because the involvement of the body's secretariat will often resolve minor procedural disputes, and when the award finally emerges, the authority of the supervising body gives added weight if and when the successful party needs to enforce it.

Another possibility is for the parties to avoid a supervising body and simply use the UNCITRAL procedure, which is readily available in various textbooks or on the internet. For example, the UNCITRAL Model Law on International Commercial Arbitration, United Nations Document A/40/17, Annex 1, is to be found in paragraph A14-001 of volume 2 of *Bernstein's handbook of arbitration and dispute resolution practice*, 4th edition (2003) (Sweet & Maxwell).

Occasionally, but very rarely, the parties will use neither a supervising body nor the UNCITRAL rules, but will simply attempt to agree their own ad hoc procedure. This is not recommended. There will inevitably be disputes about the procedure, and it will be difficult to resolve these. Most probably the courts will be approached by a disgruntled party and any hope of a straightforward arbitration will disappear.

Box 10.1: International arbitration appointing bodies

ICC	The International Court of Arbitration International Chamber of Commerce 38 Cours Albert 1er 75008 Paris France Tel. +33 1 495 32828 Fax: +33 1 495 32929 Email: arb@iccwbo.org Website: www.iccarbitration.org
LCIA	The London Court of International Arbitration 70 Fleet Street London EC4Y 1EU Tel. +44(0)20 7936 7007 Fax: +44(0)20 7936 7009 Email: ib@lcia.org Website: www.lcia.org
Swiss Chambers of Commerce	(Basle, Berne, Geneva, Lausanne, Lugano and Zurich) Rules of International Arbitration Zurich Chamber of Commerce (Attention: Dr Lukas Briner, Chief Executive Officer) Bleicherweg 5 PO Box 3058 Ch-8022 Zurich Tel. +41 1 217 4050 Fax: +41 1 217 4051 Email: direktinon@zurichcci.ch Website: www.zurichcci.ch

Initiating an arbitration

A model notice requesting an ICC arbitration is given in Box 10.8 at the end of this chapter. Also see the model letter before action and the model arbitration notice given in Chapter 5.

Great care should be taken in choosing which arbitrators to propose to the other side. A party should avoid the temptation to appoint an arbitrator who has regularly acted as either engineer or lawyer for that party, because any such proposal is likely to be rejected by the other party on the basis that there is plain conflict of interest. In determining whether or not there is such a conflict of interest the parties will find useful guidance in the International Bar Association (IBA) guidelines (see Box 10.2). In choosing who to nominate, the party should aim to

Box 10.2: IBA conflict of interest guidelines

The guidelines are set out in the *IBA Arbitration and ADR Newsletter*, October 2004, volume 9, number 2, page 7 and following.

The International Bar Association (IBA) issued in 2004 its *Guidelines on conflicts of interest in international arbitration*. These enable the parties and potential arbitrators to determine whether there is any conflict of interest applying to the appointment of a particular person as an arbitrator for a dispute. It contains red, orange and green lists, covering various possible relationships that might exist between a proposed arbitrator and one or other of the parties to the dispute. For example, if the proposed arbitrator regularly advises the party which wishes to appoint him, then this would fall within the non-waivable red list. By contrast, a proposed arbitrator who has merely previously published a general opinion in a legal journal concerning an issue arising in the arbitration would ordinarily fall within the green list.

International Bar Association
271 Regent Street
London
W1B 2AQ
Tel. +44(0)20 762 9109
Fax: +44(0)20 7409 0456
Website: www.ibanet.org

propose someone with the requisite skills (whether technical, legal or both), availability, language skills, and a reputation for producing an award promptly.

Where international supervisory bodies such as the ICC or LCIA are stipulated in the arbitration clause, generally the procedure is that for most disputes a panel of three arbitrators is to be appointed. (A sole arbitrator suffices for smaller projects.) Each party nominates one arbitrator, and these two nominees then agree the chairperson of the tribunal. The IBA guidelines state in item 4.5.1 that it is a 'green list' situation (that is, there is no appearance of, and no actual, conflict of interest) where a party, while considering whether or not to appoint an arbitrator, makes initial contact with him or her in order to discuss availability and qualifications to serve, or as to the names of possible candidates for a chairperson. Of course, there can be no discussion of the merits or procedural aspects of the dispute.

Conducting the arbitration
Appointing legal and technical advisors
Soon after the sole arbitrator or panel of arbitrators has been appointed, the tribunal will ask the parties for their views as regards the conduct

of the arbitral procedure. By this stage each party ought to have taken a policy decision as to whether or not it intends to instruct lawyers to represent it. Big companies, whether the purchaser or contractor, often have in-house legal expertise and so are able to conduct arbitrations without involving outside assistance. For most other parties serious consideration should be given to engaging lawyers experienced in arbitration – points arise where the opposition, with the benefit of legal expertise, is able to secure an advantage by reason of the non-represented party's lack of familiarity with the legal processes of arbitration.

If a party decides to seek legal help, it will usually approach a firm of solicitors (or their equivalent, e.g. attorneys in American law firms) to advise and represent it. Such firms may then choose to carry out the advocacy themselves or else to engage barristers (or their equivalent, e.g. advocates in Scotland) for pleading and presenting the case. In international disputes there is no restriction on a party, if it so chooses, directly instructing a barrister to advise and represent it. Even within England and Wales this is now generally possible through the process of Direct Professional Access and similar schemes (see Chapter 3).

Pleadings
In most arbitrations, pleadings of some kind are necessary, in which each party sets out in writing the nature of its case. If the ICC arbitration rules apply then, by Article 18 in those rules, the first step after the appointment of the tribunal is for the terms of reference to be drawn up, summarising the parties' respective positions and, usually, formulating a list of issues to be determined. Pleadings are then exchanged in the usual way. The claiming party, the 'claimant', sets out its position in its statement of case, and the other party, generally called the 'respondent', then produces its statement of defence, or defence and counterclaim (where there is a cross-claim). The claimant then serves its reply and, if necessary, defence to counterclaim. Since arbitrations are confined to the parties who have entered into the contract that contains the arbitration clause, there are usually only two parties involved in exchange of pleadings. In rare cases, if the particular rules allow, or by agreement between the parties, a third party may be added (with its consent) where there is a good reason; for example, Article 4 of the Swiss Rules for International Arbitration caters for consolidation of two sets of arbitral proceedings or for the participation of a third party.

Exchange of documents
Generally, international arbitrations will involve the parties exchanging lists of relevant documents upon which they rely, with the opportunity to inspect and make copies of documents. This procedure can often generate squabbles as to whether a party has made available all the documents it ought to have done. The incidence of such disputes is reduced where the IBA rules of evidence are used (see Box 10.3).

Box 10.3: IBA rules of evidence

The International Bar Association *Rules on the taking of evidence in international commercial arbitration* were issued in June 1999. The rules provide a mechanism for dealing with matters such as documents, witnesses of fact, expert witnesses and inspections, as well as for the conduct of evidentiary hearings. The rules are conveniently set out in *Bernstein's handbook of arbitration and dispute resolution practice*, 4th edition, volume 2, section A38 (2003) (Sweet & Maxwell).

Gathering evidence (witness statements, experts reports, etc.)
Other than where there is a simple point of law at issue (for example, a dispute as to the meaning of a clause in the contract), an arbitration will generally involve a variety of legal and factual questions. In order for a tribunal to determine such factual questions it will need to be supplied with witness statements in advance, so that, where necessary, persons to be cross-examined at a hearing may be identified. Arbitrators have a variety of preferences as to how they wish witness statements to be presented. For a complex dispute, a convenient approach is to ensure that each witness statement contains the following elements:

(1) a recent photograph of the witness (so that the tribunal can recall who the witness was, having heard a great many in the case)
(2) bullet points of what the witness intends to establish
(3) a summary of the evidence in the statement
(4) the statement itself
(5) a CV, where this is relevant (e.g. to demonstrate that the witness has a relevant professional qualification).

Preparations for the hearing
A variety of aids may be required to assist the tribunal during the hearing, including:

(1) agreed chronology of events
(2) agreed list of persons involved in the contract
(3) agreed list of issues to be determined in the arbitration (in the ICC procedure this list is in the terms of reference)
(4) opening written submissions, accompanied by legal authorities which have been marked in the margin to identify relevant passages
(5) bundles of relevant documents in chronological order, paginated throughout – if there are many files, there should be a core bundle of key documents.

The order for directions will generally include the tribunal's requirements as regards the various aids it wishes to receive in advance of the hearing so that its preparation is focused on the real issues, and so that it can understand the material put before it. Where, for example, the contract runs to many volumes because of a large number of schedules, specifications and appendices, these can usefully be reduced in size to A5 format so that the parties and the tribunal have a less burdensome bundle of material to take to the hearing. It is also common for submissions and statements to be copied onto CD ROMS and supplied to all concerned in this convenient format, in addition to the paper version.

Arbitration hearing
Since each day of hearing incurs very substantial costs, it is in the interests of both parties that the time for the hearing be strictly limited. Generally, arbitrators from an Anglo-American common law tradition are more sympathetic to applications for lengthy hearings, while tribunals from civil law jurisdictions (such as France) are reluctant to agree to a hearing extending much beyond a week. There are a variety of techniques which can be employed to reduce the length of a hearing. For example, all submissions may be confined to paper, both as regards opening and closing submissions. This leaves the hearing itself for dealing with oral examination of witnesses of fact or expertise. Often, the arrangement will be that each party is allocated half of the available time, to use as it chooses. This is sometimes termed a 'chess-clock' arrangement. Since witness statements will invariably stand as evidence-in-chief, this means that the time may be employed for cross-examination by the opposing side, or subsequent re-examination by the party calling for the witness. Arrangements for the evidence to be transcribed also speeds up the procedure, since a witness need not speak at the pace at which the slowest arbitrator is able to write. A transcript also avoids subsequent disputes about precisely what was said.

Another technique for making the most efficient use of the hearing time is so-called 'witness conferencing'. This may be conducted in various ways, but the usual procedure is for like experts from both sides to be made available to the tribunal at the same time, so that there may be a direct exchange of their views on the matters where they differ (as identified from their joint report).

Evidence by video link
It is increasingly common for witnesses, for whom attendance at the hearing would be greatly inconvenient, to give their evidence by video link. For example, it may be that a particular commissioning engineer is at a crucial stage of work on a project on a different continent and so the party calling him does not wish to put him (or his current employers, if he has left the employment of the party using him) to the inconvenience of travelling a great distance to give what may be only a few hours of evidence. In such circumstances it is often easy to arrange a video link (see Box 10.4). English barristers are often familiar with this process. It is commonly used in English criminal trials where vulnerable witnesses give evidence to the court.

Challenging and enforcing the award
Although arbitral awards, particularly those subject to the supervision of an international body such as the ICC or LCIA, are generally complied

> **Box 10.4:** Video conferencing
>
> The Bar Council of England and Wales has a video conference studio at:
>
> 289–293 High Holborn
> London
> WC1V 7HZ
> Tel. 020 7242 1289
> Email: jbradley@barcouncil.org.uk
> Website: www.londonvideoconferencing.com
>
> These facilities may be hired by members of the public.

with by the parties, it does sometimes happen that the losing party wishes to challenge the award or otherwise refuses to implement it. In such circumstances there is assistance from a number of international conventions, such as the New York Convention of 1958 for the Recognition and Enforcement of Foreign Arbitral Awards. Over 125 sovereign states are signatories to that convention, and the courts of those countries are obliged to defer to the arbitral jurisdiction whenever an action is brought under a contract containing an arbitration clause (see Article II of the New York Convention). Further, it obliges the courts of signatory states to enforce a foreign award without reviewing the merits of the arbitrators' decision (Article V). There are certain specified defences, such as where the tribunal has exceeded its jurisdiction or failed to give the complaining party a proper opportunity to present its case.

A recent example of the reluctance of English courts to interfere in international arbitrations is found in the House of Lords' Decision in *Lesotho Highlands Development Authority* v. *Impreglio SpA and Others*, *The Times*, 6th July 2005 (see Box 10.5).

Arbitration in China

Chinese government policy is to encourage international disputes to be resolved by way of arbitration rather than by reference to Chinese or foreign courts. The Chinese Arbitration Act 1994/5 is based, as with many national arbitration acts, on the UNCITRAL Model Law. This provides, among other things, that if there is a valid arbitration clause in an agreement, a court will refuse to entertain proceedings and will send a dispute to arbitration (Article 5 of Chapter 1). Enforcement may be somewhat uncertain because of the reluctance of certain Chinese courts to enforce awards which may conflict with the local economic interest.

The two principal arbitration bodies in China are the China International Economic and Trade Arbitration Commission (CIETAC) and the China Maritime Arbitration Commission (CMAC). It is the former which is relevant for the purposes of engineering and construction disputes. CIETAC has its own published rules of procedure (the

Box 10.5: *Lesotho Highlands Development Authority* v. *Impreglio SpA and Others* (6th July 2005) HL

Contractors were engaged to construct a dam in Lesotho. The law of the contract was that of the Kingdom of Lesotho and the currency of account was to be the local currency, the maloti. The contract excluded any right of appeal on a point of law under section 69 of the English Arbitration Act 1996, and provided for ICC arbitration. The contractors successfully claimed for increased costs by way of an ICC arbitration in London. Since the value of the maloti had fallen heavily, the arbitrators, in reliance on section 48(4) of the 1996 Act, made their award in the contractors' own currencies converted from the maloti at a rate prescribed in the contract, which predated the maloti's collapse. The employer objected. The House of Lords held that a mere error of law by the arbitrators did not amount to an excess of power under the 1996 Act so as to allow the court to interfere with the award. Lord Steyn said, among other things, that a major purpose of the 1996 Act had been to reduce drastically the extent of intervention of courts in the arbitral process.

CIETAC Rules), and operates in a similar fashion to the ICC in Paris. However, the parties are allowed to agree to use procedural rules other than those of CIETAC. CIETAC arbitrators are permitted to act as conciliators as well, provided the parties agree (Article 37 of the CIETAC Rules). CIETAC considers this combination of conciliation and arbitration to be one of its attractive features. As arbitrations progress, the tribunal may actively encourage conciliation. It is rare for ad hoc arbitrations, outside of the CIETAC or CMAC procedures, to occur in China.

China is a signatory to the New York Convention. Further, China has entered into a multitude of bilateral treaties relating to arbitrations and award enforcement. The CIETAC Rules reflect internationally accepted procedures. They permit foreigners to be appointed as arbitrators in China, and many such persons are members of the CIETAC panel. Generally, foreign businesses consider CIETAC to give good value for money. Chinese is specified as the arbitration language by the CIETAC Rules. Generally, all documentation (including correspondence, submissions, etc.) is required to be translated into Chinese. Chinese is also the language adopted for all arbitral hearings. However, the parties may agree on a foreign language. The parties may choose either a sole arbitrator or a panel of three (consisting of a president and two others, each appointed by one of the parties).

A CIETAC arbitration is commenced once the claimant has submitted an application, chosen an arbitrator from the commission's list and paid the appropriate fee. The application should include a statement of the claimant's case and supporting documents. The procedural rules permit the arbitrators to carry out investigations, gather evidence, summon witnesses and consult experts (both Chinese and foreign). Hearing dates are fixed by the CIETAC secretariat after consultation with the arbitral tribunal (but rarely with the parties). The hearing procedure is broadly similar to that used in English arbitrations. Each party puts its case orally, calling witnesses as necessary. Questions are then put by the tribunal to the witnesses, the parties and their representatives. In addition, each party may question the other. Legal submissions then follow. Broadly, the CIETAC Rules permit foreign lawyers to represent parties. CIETAC has its permanent seat in Beijing and most hearings are held there, but there are CIETAC arbitration branches in other cities, such as Shanghai and Shenzhen.

The tribunal may issue interim or partial awards, as well as the final award itself. An award is, generally, not subject to judicial or other review. Once CIETAC has issued an arbitral award, it must be implemented within whatever time period is stipulated by the tribunal. Since 2000, CIETAC has dealt with more than 3500 arbitrations. It is now the biggest arbitration body in the world and continues to grow at an impressive rate.

Arbitration in Singapore

Broadly, the Singaporean legal system is based upon the English common law, and its arbitration laws reflect the English approach. Arbitrations are governed by the Singapore Arbitration Act 1953, amended in 1980 to take account of the English Arbitration Act 1979. The Singapore Rules of the Supreme Court, Order 69, deals with arbitration proceedings. Arbitrations with an international element are governed by the Singaporean International Arbitration Act 2002, which replaced the International Arbitration Act 1995. This allows the parties to choose to exclude application of the UNCITRAL Model Law, which otherwise applies, with the exception of Chapter VIII on recognition and enforcement of awards. However, the UNCITRAL Model Law always remains subject to the provisions of the 2002 Act.

Any arbitral award made in Singapore may be appealed, provided the parties consent, or leave is granted by the court. The parties may agree to exclude such appeals. Singapore is a signatory to the 1958 New York Convention and the 1965 Washington Convention (which provides for the resolution of disputes between a state or state entity and a private party). Further, the 1958 Reciprocal Enforcement of Commonwealth Judgments Act, applying to judgments of superior courts of the UK and other Commonwealth countries, extended reciprocity to Singaporean judgments (including arbitration awards).

The Singapore International Arbitration Centre (SIAC) was established in 1991. It administers a panel of over 130 arbitrators operating in the Association of South East Asian Nations (ASEAN) area, and a further international panel consisting of about 70 members from countries outside the ASEAN area. Its website is www.siac.org.sg. An indication of the popularity of Singapore as an arbitration centre is given by the fact that the ICC's 2002 figures show Singapore was expressly chosen by parties for 14 ICC arbitrators.

Arbitration in Malaysia

As with Singapore, the Malaysian legal system is based upon the English common law. The English Arbitration Act 1950 strongly influenced the Malaysian Arbitration Act 1952. The 1952 Act was revised in 1972. Also refer to the 1980 Rules of the High Court. A court may direct an arbitrator to state any question of law as a 'special case' for the court's consideration during the course of an arbitration. Malaysia has adopted the UNCITRAL Model Law.

Section 34 of the 1952 Act minimises court interference in international arbitrations. Thus, the 1952 Act does not apply to arbitrations administered by the Regional Centre for Arbitration Kuala Lumpur (RCAKL), and also those held under the UNCITRAL Rules, as well as those under the International Convention for the Settlement of Investment Disputes (ICSID). Judicial authority confirms that foreigners may act as arbitrators and advocates in arbitrations within Malaysia. As with Singapore, Malaysia is a signatory to the New York and Washington Conventions, and the Reciprocal Enforcement of Judgments Act 1958. In 1999, the RCAKL handled 19 new international arbitrations. This compares with four in 1993.

Arbitration in South Korea

Procedure is governed by the Commercial Arbitration Rules of 1973 (and subsequently amended). If parties fail to agree otherwise, the Rules apply. The parties may choose the law applicable, but if they fail to then Korean law provides that the law of the place where the offer to make the contract was made should apply. Foreign lawyers may act as advocates in arbitrations in Korea. South Korea is a signatory to the 1958 New York Convention and the 1967 Washington Convention. In 1999 Korea's KCAB arbitration centre handled 14 new international arbitrations.

The Arbitration Act which came into force on 31st December 1999 adopts much of the UNCITRAL Model Law, and also reflects aspects of the procedure from institutions such as the ICC and LCIA. Consequently, its effect is that the courts reject actions where there is a valid arbitration agreement in place. The South Korean courts have shown an awareness of the desire of international parties for courts to avoid interference in the arbitral process.

Arbitration in Australia

International arbitration in Australia is governed by the 1974 International Arbitration Act, amended in 2004. This Act provides that the UNCITRAL Model Law shall have the force of law in Australia. Thus, it is similar to the equivalent New Zealand legislation. Both the Australian and New Zealand Acts expressly exclude arbitrators' liability for negligence in carrying out their functions as the tribunal. Further, the Australian Act supplements the Model Law by containing, in sections 22–27, a variety of optional provisions which the parties may choose to adopt, provided they do so in writing. This includes, for example, consolidation of arbitration proceedings and payment of interest and costs. By section 21 of the 1974 Act, the parties may choose to opt out of the UNCITRAL Model Law altogether.

The UNCITRAL Rules are recommended by both of the leading Australian arbitration bodies, the Institute of Arbitrators and Mediators Australia (IAMA) and the Australian Centre for International Commercial Arbitration (ACICA). ACICA and IAMA have lists of experienced arbitration practitioners. Although the number of international arbitrations taking place in Australia is growing, in 2002 there was only one ICC arbitration where the parties had specifically chosen Australia as the venue. There were, of course, many other arbitrations where the ICC was not the supervising body.

Arbitration in Taiwan

The primary legislation is the 1961 Commercial Arbitration Law, as amended in 1982 and 1986. Parties may choose the law applicable to the procedure, but if they failed to choose then the 1961 Act and the Non-Litigation Acts (which govern procedure) apply. Article 5 of the 1961 Act restricts the choice of arbitrators to the ranks of the persons recognised as competent in the law or having a professional knowledge of a particular trade and who are noted for impartiality and integrity. Rules as to representation are relaxed, and parties may appoint agents to present their cases.

Arbitration in New Zealand

The 1996 Arbitration Act is substantially based on the UNCITRAL Model Law. Broadly, arbitration practice in New Zealand is similar to that in England and Wales. The New Zealand courts, as with the English courts, recognise that the parties to arbitration agreements do not favour unnecessary interference by local courts. Of course, awards may be set aside where there has not been a fair hearing. For applications to the court for leave to appeal, one of the considerations a New Zealand court will take into account is whether the dispute is international or domestic. Under the 1996 Act the parties to an international arbitration can opt in to clause 5 and expressly choose to have that clause (which deals with leave to appeal) applied to their arbitration. If they do not so choose, then their recourse to the New Zealand courts is restricted to seeking setting aside the award on the grounds in Article 34 of the First Schedule (which deals with, for example, failure to apply the rules of natural justice).

Adjudication and dispute boards

The spread of adjudication

UK adjudication procedures are described in detail in Chapter 6. Other jurisdictions have adopted or are considering adopting similar adjudication schemes, including several Australian states, New Zealand, Texas (USA), Singapore and, more recently, Malaysia (see, for example, 'Adjudication – a new direction for construction disputes' by Robert Gaitskell, QC in the *IBA Asia Pacific Forum News*, June 2003, volume 11, number 1, pages 5–6).

Adjudication in Australia

New South Wales, Victoria and Queensland have already introduced a statutory adjudication procedure. The New South Wales Building and Construction Industry Security of Payment Act 1999 was taken into account by Singapore when the latter more recently introduced its own similarly named legislation. At present the leading New South Wales case on the adjudication procedure is *Transgrid* v. *Siemens* [2004] NSWCA 395, where the approach of the English Court of Appeal in *Bouygues* v. *Dahl-Jensen* [2000] BLR 522 was approved. The Court said that the role of an adjudicator was analogous to that of an expert by whose determination the parties had agreed to be bound. Thus, the courts of New South Wales are adopting a similar 'hands-off' approach to adjudication decisions as applies in the UK. In *Bouygues* the English Court of Appeal held that although the adjudication decision contained an error, it was an error made when the adjudicator was acting within his jurisdiction and so his decision would stand and be enforced. It is this non-interventionist approach that has made adjudication so popular in the UK, because the parties know that courts will be reluctant to interfere with an adjudication decision. As in the UK, provided the rules of natural justice are observed, and the adjudicator does not act outside of his or her jurisdiction, the likelihood is that the resulting decision will be enforced by the courts.

The New South Wales Act, like the UK legislation, applies to professional services and does not apply to residential property. However, only the party demanding progress payments may initiate adjudication (by contrast, both the UK and New Zealand allow either the employer or the contractor to commence the process).

Adjudication in New Zealand

Adjudication in New Zealand is controlled by the Construction Contracts Act 2002, which reflects the English Housing Grants, Construction and Regeneration Act 1996 as well as the 1999 Act of New South Wales, Australia. However, both the New Zealand and Australian Acts include a detailed adjudication scheme, whereas in the UK the scheme is contained in a subsequent statutory instrument.

The 2002 Act came into force on 1st April 2003 and applies to every 'construction contract' made on or after that date, even if not in writing (section 9). Unlike the UK, New Zealand residential 'construction contracts' are covered by the Act, although certain of the provisions, such as the right of an unpaid contractor to suspend work, do not then apply.

The adjudicator's powers are equivalent to those of adjudicators in England, and are much wider than those applying in Australia (see section 42(1) of the 2002 Act). By section 9, the 2002 Act applies to every construction contract (whether or not governed by New Zealand law) that relates to construction work in New Zealand.

There are certain important differences between the New Zealand and UK legislation. The New Zealand 2002 Act covers only 'construction work' and does not apply, for example, to 'advice on building, engineering...' in the way that section 104 of the English 1996 Act does. A New Zealand adjudicator is permitted 20 working days after the end of the period within which the respondent may serve its adjudication response. This is similar to the UK's period of 28 calendar days commencing with the date of the referral notice.

Interestingly, by section 40 of the New Zealand 2002 Act, there is provision for consolidation of adjudications. However, in practice few parties attempt to achieve such consolidation because of the tight time-scale. Consequently, cross-claims and successive claims are dealt with sequentially.

Adjudication in Singapore

On 1st April 2005, Singapore's Building and Construction Industry Security of Payment Act 2004 came into effect. Although this has similar objectives to the Housing Grants, Construction and Regeneration Act 1996 in England, there are a number of differences – this is because Singapore has been strongly influenced by the Australian legislation. As with the English 1996 Act, there is a statutory adjudication procedure, which supplements but does not replace any contractual right to arbitrate or litigate. A useful textbook on the 2005 Act is Chow Kok Fong's *Security of payments and construction adjudication* (2005) (LexisNexis).

Unlike the English statutory procedure, which allows for a multitude of adjudicator appointing bodies, the Singaporean 2004 Act requires any references to adjudication to be conducted through the Singapore Mediation Centre ('the Centre'). The Centre has issued its own Adjudication Procedure Rules, which are similar in a number of respects to the statutory Scheme for Construction Contracts applying in England. However, one important difference between the Singaporean and English schemes is that the entitlement in England to proceed to adjudication 'at any time' (see section 108(2)(a) of the 1996 Act) is not reflected in the Singaporean legislation.

As with all current adjudication legislation in common law jurisdictions, the Singaporean procedure is focused on dealing with disputes concerning progress payments. A claimant that contends the appropriate payment has not been made within the applicable period becomes entitled to make an adjudication application to the Centre within 7 days of that entitlement arising. Thereafter, the Centre appoints the adjudicator. The respondent is then obliged to set out its reasons for withholding payment, and to identify any cross-claim or set-off for which it contends.

The powers of the adjudicator under the Singaporean procedure are similar to those under the English Scheme for Construction Contracts. In both the adjudicator is required to conduct the adjudication in accordance with the rules of natural justice (i.e. the adjudicator must be unbiased, and both parties must be given a fair opportunity to state their case and know the other side's case).

An important difference between the English and Singaporean schemes is the statutory procedure for reviewing adjudication decisions. Any application for such a review must be made within 7 days of receipt of the decision, and in making the application the respondent is obliged to pay the amount determined in the adjudication decision to the claimant. Generally, the review will be conducted within 14 days, subject to all concerned agreeing an extension of time.

Adjudication in Hong Kong

A contractual adjudication procedure is available in Hong Kong. However, there is no statutory right to adjudicate. The Hong Kong Government's General Conditions of Contract simply permit a party to request adjudication. If the other party declines this invitation then the matter proceeds to arbitration, provided this is done within 90 days of the refusal to adjudicate. As with the English procedure, a party dissatisfied with an adjudication decision may take the matter to arbitration.

Where a party proposes to adjudicate pursuant to the Government's General Conditions of Contract, the Adjudication Rules apply, and these specify that the Hong Kong International Arbitration Centre is to control the adjudication. This includes appointing an adjudicator in the event that the parties are unable to agree upon the identity of such a person.

The Arbitration Rules further provide that where an adjudication does take place the decision must be rendered within 56 days (unlike the 28 days specified in the English statutory procedure). Since the Hong Kong International Arbitration Centre itself incurs costs in administering the process, each party is obliged to make an initial deposit of HK$50,000 to the centre within 7 days of the commencement date (the date upon which the adjudicator was appointed). The deposited sum is reviewed as the nature of the dispute is clarified.

Adjudication in Malaysia

The Malaysian Construction Industry met at a round-table discussion in Kuala Lumpur on 24th June 2003, and the outcome was a draft Construction Industry Master Plan, 2005–2015. One of the matters discussed was payment within the construction industry, and this led to an International Forum on Adjudication, held in Kuala Lumpur on 13th and 14th September 2005. The result is likely to be an early introduction of appropriate legislation, taking account of experience in Singapore, the UK and other jurisdictions which have already introduced adjudication.

Dispute boards (serial adjudication)

Background

Dispute boards (DBs) generally involve a procedure whereby a 'board' of two engineers and one lawyer is appointed at the outset of a project to deal with complaints as they arise and prevent them developing into intractable disputes. The cost of retaining such a board throughout a project is only justified where the project is reasonably big. For smaller projects, a board consisting of only one member is sometimes used, to reduce costs. The board generally visits the site three or four times a year. By immediately addressing squabbles on site, the board is generally able to prevent disputes festering and ultimately going to costly arbitration. With World Bank encouragement, the Fédération Internationale

> **Box 10.6:** ICC Dispute Board documentation
>
> - Dispute Board Member Agreement
> - Dispute Board Rules
> - Standard ICC Dispute Board Clauses

des Ingénieurs-Conseils (FIDIC) has included a DB procedure in its standard forms for some years. More recently, the ICC has produced a set of DB Rules and produced all the necessary documents for establishing an effective DB (see Box 10.6).

Since boards effectively operate by conducting serial adjudications at regular intervals throughout a project, they are becoming increasingly popular with construction industry professionals, who are now thoroughly familiar with the adjudication process from the UK and elsewhere. Consequently, usage of the DB procedure internationally is expected to grow rapidly.

Operating a dispute board
The board should be appointed at the outset of a project so that it is familiar with all the processes that occur on site. This means, for example, that it will know what work has been covered over (e.g. in foundations) even though a dispute about that work may only arise late in the project.

When the board conducts a site visit it will generally 'walk the site' to see what work is being carried out and hold a meeting with both parties to the contract to hear any complaints. If decisions need to be made, the board can do this, having held reasonably informal and brief hearings. Generally, written decisions and recommendations will be issued and, if one party or the other does not accept the outcome, the matter may proceed to arbitration. This rarely happens.

Usually, the board continues until substantial completion of the works, and then remains available to the parties if they wish it to visit site and make any further decisions. Otherwise, it simply terminates altogether when the project is complete. Unfortunately, some parties, hoping to reduce the costs of maintaining the board, only appoint it well into the project, when a dispute is looming, and then attempt to terminate its activities prior to substantial completion of the works. This reduces the effectiveness of the board because it does not have a full knowledge of the work carried out and the circumstances in which it was done. Nevertheless, a board operating for only part of the project period is better than no board.

Mediation and early neutral evaluation
The differences between mediation and early neutral evaluation
Mediation is an increasingly popular procedure in which a neutral third party helps the disputing parties to reach a deal. In the UK this procedure is generally 'facilitative', so that at no time does the mediator publicly express any views as to the strengths or weaknesses of the parties' cases.

This is what marks mediation out from the procedures of conciliation and early neutral evaluation (ENE). In conciliation and ENE the third party is 'evaluative' and, in the presence of both parties, will express a view as to what the outcome of the dispute should be. With conciliation this expression of a view (which may be binding) generally follows a form of mediation, while with ENE there is simply a brief hearing followed by the giving of the evaluation. (See Chapter 7 for details of the mediation process and Chapter 9 for details of the ENE process.)

There can be significant differences between the mediation procedures used in different jurisdictions. For example, whereas in Europe it is common to have an entirely facilitative process, taking no more than one day in most cases, in South East Asian jurisdictions, such as Hong Kong, it is not unusual to have mediations stretching over several days, if not weeks, and ending with a determinative process. Accordingly, when parties set about agreeing and implementing a 'mediation' process they need to be fully aware of what each other understands by the term, and any mediator they appoint should be fully apprised of the parties' expectations as regards how the process should be conducted.

An ENE hearing is similar in many respects to a summary judgment hearing before a judge, with the matter being dealt with in one day, or sometimes less. The evaluator will then issue an evaluation, generally in writing.

Initiating a mediation

Parties wishing to mediate may either contact an appointing and supervising body, such as the Centre for Effective Dispute Resolution (CEDR) (see Box 10.7) or, if they can agree on the identity of the mediator, contact him or her directly. The ICC in Paris also provides mediators. Two agreements then need to be made: one with the mediator, as regards his or her fees and the terms upon which the mediation will be carried out, and a second between the parties, as regards the mediation procedure they have agreed upon. For example, it is common to stipulate in such an agreement that there is no binding deal until there is a written signed document. This avoids the uncertainty which could otherwise arise with an entirely oral compromise in the context of a day of negotiations.

Box 10.7: Centre for Effective Dispute Resolution

CEDR Solve
International Dispute Resolution Centre
70 Fleet Street
London
EC4Y 1EU
Tel. +44(0)20 7536 6060
Fax: +44(0)20 7536 6061
Email: info@cedr-solve.com
Website: www.cedr-solve.com

Since international mediations generally involve parties from two different countries, it sometimes happens that they are unable to agree on a mediator from either of the countries from which they come. In such circumstances a mediator from a third country is a suitable compromise choice. Thus, English mediators often prove popular where there are disputes between, say, an Asian party and a Scandinavian party.

Expert determination

The ICC's International Centre for Expertise is able to appoint and administer expert determinations for international disputes. If the parties so choose, the ICC will make an appointment but then leave it to the parties and the appointed expert to continue the process without supervision. However, if the parties prefer, the ICC will supervise the process throughout, until the determination has been issued. (See Chapter 8 for details of the expert determination process.)

Conclusion

Controlling the dispute procedure

Since international disputes involve, by their very nature, parties from two different countries and, potentially, two quite different cultures, it can often be difficult to reach any agreement as to a dispute resolution procedure once the parties have fallen out. For this reason it is essential that the contract, drafted at a time when both parties are being co-operative, sets out in detail the procedure to be adopted when a dispute arises.

As discussed in Chapter 2, a layered dispute resolution clause offers many benefits, since it allows the parties to attempt to resolve their dispute with 'soft' procedures, such as negotiations between senior management followed where necessary by mediation, rather than simply proceeding directly to a 'hard' procedure such as arbitration. Since mediation, for example, has a very high success rate, using it allows the parties to keep control of the process and minimise costs and, where the mediation works, generally end the dispute on reasonably good terms.

Making the best use of the outcome

If it does become necessary to begin implementing a dispute resolution clause, the parties should attempt to secure a deal whenever the opportunity arises. For example, if a specific dispute is dealt with by expert determination, the moment that result is obtained the parties should see if any other disputes can also be resolved amicably at that time. Similarly, if a DB is appointed, whenever a decision or recommendation is produced, it should be used as an opportunity to resolve any other outstanding matters. In this way the parties will retain control of the dispute resolution processes and minimise their costs. When parties fail to do this, and, in effect, use a dispute resolution clause as a means of conducting low-level warfare, both parties will ultimately suffer. First, the costs will be vast. Second, future business between the parties will become impossible. Third, even when a decision is obtained, at great expense, from the arbitral tribunal, there is the possibility of further skirmishes over challenges and enforcement, with their cost consequences. In summary, parties should pay great attention to the drafting of any dispute resolution clause, and if circumstances arise where it has to be used, they should do their best to make the most of each stage in the process to avoid an engineering project simply turning into a war of attrition from which no one will benefit.

Box 10.8: Model notice requesting an ICC arbitration

CONTRACTOR INC.

– v –

SUPPLIER LTD

REQUEST FOR ICC ARBITRATION

1. **Introduction**

1.1 This Request for Arbitration is submitted pursuant to Article 4 of the Rules of Arbitration of the International Chamber of Commerce (1998) by the Claimant, Contractor Inc., in respect of the disputes summarised in this document.

1.2 We confirm that we are authorised by the Claimant to submit this request.

2. **The Parties**

2.1 *The Claimant:* Contractor Inc. is a company incorporated in England. Its principal office is at:

Contractor House
Westminster Road
London
WC1 1AB
United Kingdom
Tel. +44 (0)1234 5678
Fax: +44 (0)1234 5679

2.2 The Claimant is represented by:

Solicitors LLP
Shoe Lane
London
EC1 1AB
United
Kingdom
Tel. +44 (0)207 123 4567
Fax: +44 (0)207 123 4569
Ref: AB/CD

2.3   *The Respondent:* Supplier Ltd ('Supplier') is a company incorporated in the USA. Its offices are at:

Supplier Incorporated
Supplier House
PO Box 1234
Texas
USA
Tel. +1 123 456 7890
Fax: +1 123 456 7891

2.4   The Contract (defined below) provides that contractual notices shall be given in writing and either personally delivered, sent by express air courier service, or sent by telex or telefax.

3.   **Relevant Agreement and Agreement to Arbitrate**

3.1   The relevant Contract (the 'Contract') is set out in the following documents:
(a)   Purchase Order No. 1234 dated 1 January 2001 (the 'Purchase Order');
(b)   Terms and Conditions of Contract (the 'Terms and Conditions') attached to the Purchase Order; and
(c)   Technical specification ABC-1234567 (the 'Specification').

3.2   Clause 22.2 of the Terms and Conditions of the Contract provides:

> 'Any dispute, controversy or claim arising out of or relating to this Agreement shall be finally determined and settled by arbitration. Such arbitration shall take place in London, England pursuant to the Rules of Conciliation and Arbitration of the International Chamber of Commerce (hereinafter the "appointing authority"). The panel of arbitrators shall consist of three persons whose proceedings will be conducted in the English language. Judgment upon the decision and any award made by the arbitrators may be entered by any court having jurisdiction thereof.'

4.   **Number and Nomination of Arbitrator**

4.1   Clause 22.2 of the Terms and Conditions of the Contract, as set out in paragraph 3.2 above, provides that any disputes shall be decided by three arbitrators.

4.2   The Claimant nominates its arbitrator as:

Mr Arbitrator
Arbitration Chambers
London
EC1 1AB
United Kingdom
Tel. +44 (0)207 444 4567
Fax: +44 (0)207 444 4569

5.   **Place of Arbitration**

Clause 22.2 of the Terms and Conditions of the Contract provides that the arbitration shall take place in London, England.

6.   **Language of the Arbitration**

6.1   Clause 22.2 of the Terms and Conditions of the Contract provides that the proceedings will be conducted in the English language.

7.   **Applicable Law**

7.1   Clause 22.1 of the Terms and Conditions of the Contract provides:

'This Agreement shall be governed by and construed and enforced in accordance with the laws of England.'

8.   **Nature and Circumstances of the Dispute**

8.1   Pursuant to the Contract, the Respondent agreed to supply the Claimant with metering stations for the measurement of crude oil and bunker exports (the 'metering system') at an on-shore oil-loading terminal in the Middle East. The purchase price was US$5,000,000.

8.2   The metering system installation was completed in or about September 2002. Commissioning commenced from October 2002. In the course of commissioning, defects came to light in the metering system, including, amongst others, defective valves and problems with the prover loop.

8.3   The Claimant brought the problems of the prover loop and the fact that the valves were defective to the attention of the Respondent. Despite numerous requests from the Claimant to do so, the Respondent failed to remedy all or any of the defects that had been identified.

8.4   The Claimant thereupon took steps to rectify the problems in consultation with the Employer. On 29 July 2003, the

Employer completed the replacement of some 36 defective valves supplied by the Respondent pursuant to the Contract. Between April and June 2003, the Employer replaced the prover loop. In August 2003, the metering system was successfully commissioned.

8.5   The total costs incurred by the Employer, and charged to and paid by the Claimant to the Employer, in respect of the replacement of defective valves and the rectification of the prover loop, amounted to US$3,000,000.

9   Relief Sought by the Claimant

9.1   The Claimant seeks:

9.1.1   an award in respect of the losses arising from the Respondent's failure to replace the defective valves or to rectify the prover loop, amounting to US$3,000,000;

9.1.2   an award of interest in respect of any amounts found owing to it;

9.1.3   an award of costs, pursuant to Article 31 of the ICC Rules;

9.1.4   all and any such other relief as the Tribunal determines is appropriate.

9.2   The Claimant reserves the right to amend and/or amplify the basis of its claim or the relief sought in its Statement of Case to follow.

10.   Advance Payment of the Administrative Expenses

10.1   Pursuant to Article 4.4 and Appendix III of the ICC Rules, the Claimant encloses a cheque for US$2,500.

21 September 2005

Solicitors LLP

**For and on behalf of
Contractor Inc.**

11. Immediate help

Jonathan Selby

The court system and useful resources

This chapter sets out some explanation about the court system, precedent and law reporting. It also identifies some useful reference points for finding lawyers and the relevant law.

The court system

The court system in England and Wales is divided between civil and criminal courts.

Criminal courts not only try matters such as murder and robbery but are also responsible for hearing prosecutions under environmental, waste management and health and safety legislation. Depending upon the seriousness of the crime, such prosecutions will be tried in the magistrates' court or the Crown court – with the more serious offences being tried in the Crown court. For further information about the criminal courts and the appropriate procedure, refer to one of the two core texts: *Archbold: Criminal pleading, evidence and practice* (Sweet & Maxwell) or *Blackstone's criminal practice* (Oxford University Press). Each is published annually.

The civil courts try disputes between private parties, such as claims for payment of invoices and claims for compensation. In broad terms, claims for less than £50,000 are tried in the county courts whereas claims for more than £50,000 are tried in the High Court. All civil courts are governed by the Civil Procedure Rules. For further information about the civil courts and the appropriate procedure, refer to one of two core texts: *The White Book* (Sweet & Maxwell) or *The Civil Court Practice* (*The Green Book*) (Butterworths Law). Each is published annually.

For construction and engineering disputes, there is a specialist Technology and Construction Court. Its main base is in London but it also has regional branches throughout the country (at both county court and High Court level). Because only judges with appropriate experience in construction and engineering disputes can sit in the Technology and Construction Court, this generally means that parties can have greater confidence that their disputes will be tried by judges who understand the issues in their case. As a result, cases can be tried a lot quicker. Further information about the Technology and Construction Court can be found in the TCC Court Guide, which is available at www.hmcourts-service. gov.uk/docs/tcc_guide.htm.

If a party wishes to appeal a decision of either the High Court or the Crown court, it has to appeal to the Court of Appeal. Thereafter, if a party is still not satisfied with the decision of the Court of Appeal, it can attempt to appeal to the House of Lords – the highest court in England and Wales.

The rules relating to appeals from decisions of the county court or magistrates' court are more varied and are outside the scope of this book. However, although such appeals are not decided by the Court of Appeal in the first instance, they can subsequently be appealed to the Court of Appeal and ultimately to the House of Lords in appropriate circumstances.

Precedent

The doctrine of precedent is the process by which the courts look at previously decided cases and apply their decisions to existing disputes. For a detailed explanation on the doctrine of precedent, refer to *Precedent in English Law* by Sir Rupert Cross and J.W. Harris (Clarendon Press). However, set out here is an overview of the doctrine of precedent.

In general terms, the enunciation of the reason or principle upon which a question before a court has been decided is binding as a precedent. The underlying principle – or the basis upon which the previous case was decided – is called the *'ratio decidendi'*. By contrast, comments in judgments which do not form the basis upon which the previous case was decided are called *'obiter dicta'* and are not binding as precedent.

Lower courts are bound to follow the decisions of higher courts. So, for example, the Court of Appeal cannot derogate from decisions of the House of Lords and the High Court cannot derogate from decisions of the Court of Appeal. Conversely, higher courts are not bound to follow the decisions of lower courts. So, for example, the Court of Appeal will not consider itself bound by the decision of a High Court judge. Nevertheless, higher courts will often have regard to decisions of lower courts, especially when points of law have not been considered elsewhere.

As to how the doctrine of precedent applies to courts of equal jurisdiction, different rules apply depending upon whether the court is the House of Lords, the Court of Appeal or a court of first instance (such as the High Court). The House of Lords will not depart from its own previous decisions unless it is right to do so; for example, because too rigid adherence to precedent may lead to injustice in a particular case or may unduly restrict the proper development of the law. Similarly, the Court of Appeal will follow its own previous decisions unless:

(1) there are two or more conflicting decisions of the Court of Appeal – in which case it is bound to decide which to follow, or
(2) its previous decision is not consistent with a decision of the House of Lords, or
(3) if its previous decision is *'per incuriam'*.

A decision is *per incuriam* where the court has acted in ignorance of a House of Lords' decision or in ignorance of a previous decision of its own or in ignorance of a statute or rule having statutory force.

As to how the doctrine of precedent applies where one judge in a court of first instance (e.g. the High Court) is considering the decision of a judge of equal jurisdiction, such courts are not strictly bound by their previous decisions, although generally, as a matter of judicial comity, the second judge will follow the decision of the first judge unless he or she is convinced that the judgment was wrong.

The doctrine of precedent only applies in relation to cases in England and Wales. Cases from other jurisdictions (for example, Scotland, Australia and other Commonwealth countries) are often cited to the English courts. However, these decisions are not binding as a matter of precedent and are only of persuasive authority.

Law reporting

In order for the doctrine of precedent to work in practice, cases have to be reported. Traditionally, cases were reported in bound volumes of the Law Reports. However, with the growth of the internet, many cases are reported online long before they even reach the press. The final section of this chapter identifies some libraries and websites where various law reports can be found. However, before reading that section, it is important to understand how the courts view various forms of law reporting.

The 'official' series of law reports is called the 'Law Reports' and is published by the Incorporated Council of Law Reporting for England and Wales. This series includes the Appeal Cases, the Queen's Bench Division and the Weekly Law Reports. Where a case is cited in the Law Reports, a copy from the relevant report should be provided.

If a case is not cited in the Law Reports, it may be reported in the All England Reports. In such circumstances, the All England Reports should be cited to the court.

Otherwise, there are numerous other specialist types of law report, such as the Building Law Reports, Lloyd's Law Reports and the Professional Negligence Law Reports. If a case is not cited in either the Law Reports series or the All England Reports, it is appropriate to refer to the version contained in these reports.

Only if a particular case is not cited in any of the published law reports is it appropriate to refer to cases which have been reported online or to rely on a transcript of the relevant judgment.

References

Where a case is cited, a reference to where it can be located ought usually to be provided after the case name. The reference is normally provided with an abbreviation which relates to the relevant report. For example, WLR relates to the Weekly Law Reports and BLR relates to the Building Law Reports. A full list of all abbreviations is available at: www.legalabbrevs.cardiff.ac.uk.

The reference will also refer to the year of the report, the volume of the report and the page number within a particular volume. Therefore, a reference to [2005] 2 BLR 327 means that the case can be found in volume 2 of the 2005 Building Law Reports at page 327.

In addition, a method of neutral citation has been introduced. However, the neutral citation reference does not actually assist in helping someone find a copy of the relevant decision. All it does is provide a unique reference code and identifies which court the decision was made in and the year in which it was made. Some of the relevant abbreviations include EWHL (House of Lords), EWCA (Civ) (Court of Appeal, Civil Division) and EWHC (High Court). EWHC references also identify in which division of the High Court the decision was made. Hence, references to EWHC (TCC) relate to the Technology and Construction Court. The prefix 'EW' refers to the jurisdiction of England and Wales.

Reference sources
Appointing a lawyer
If a party to a dispute does not know any lawyers and is unable to obtain a personal recommendation from an associate, there are two useful reference points: legal directories and the Law Society.

The main directories are those produced by Chambers and Partners and the *Legal 500*, which can often be obtained at major libraries. The websites for these directories are:

* www.chambersandpartners.com
* www.legal500.com

The Law Society also has a system for recommending firms of solicitors. Its contact details are:

Ipsley Court
Berrington House
Redditch
Worcestershire
B98 0TD
Tel. 0870 606 6575
Website: www.lawsociety.org.uk/choosingandusing.law

Legal resources
There is a growing number of websites which contain legal resources. However, many of them simply contain electronic versions of the bound law reports. Before identifying some of the more useful websites, this section identifies some of the key texts that deal with construction law and the libraries where paper legal resources are available.

Major construction law textbooks
The three major textbooks which deal specifically with construction law are:

* *Keating on Building Contracts* (Sweet & Maxwell)
* *Hudson's Building and Engineering Contracts* (Sweet & Maxwell)
* *Emden's Construction Law* (Butterworths Tolley).

For the field of arbitration, key textbooks include:

* *Arbitration Law*, by Robert Merkin (Lloyd's of London Press)

- *Commercial Arbitration*, by Sir Michael Mustill and Stewart Boyd (Butterworths)
- *Russell on Arbitration* (Sweet & Maxwell).

Libraries
Not all libraries are well resourced with law books and law reports. However, the following two public libraries have good collections of legal texts:

The British Library
St Pancras
96 Euston Road
London
NW1 2DB
Tel. 0207 412 7332
Website: www.bl.uk

Holborn Library
32–38 Theobald's Road
London
WC1X 8PA
Tel. 0207 974 6345

Members of professional institutions (such as the Institution of Civil Engineers) should also investigate what resources their own libraries have.

Non-subscription websites
There are many websites which provide a variety of information for free.

For case reports:

- www.bailii.org – for general case reports (except House of Lords' decisions)
- www.publications.parliament.uk/pa/ld199697/ldjudgmt/ldjudgmt.htm – for House of Lords' decisions
- www.scotcourts.gov.uk – for Scottish decisions

For adjudication cases:

- www.adjudication.co.uk

For the Civil Procedure Rules:

- www.dca.gov.uk/civil/procrules_fin/index.htm

For statutes:

- www.opsi.gov.uk/legislation/index.htm

Subscription websites
In addition to the free websites, there are a number of subscription-based websites which provide a variety of additional services (such as search facilities) that are not readily available on the non-subscription websites. These sites also contain electronic versions of law reports that are published in hard copy. Such sites include:

- www.lawtel.com – contains a number of reported and unreported cases
- www.justis.com – contains the Law Reports series
- www.lloydslawreports.com – contains not only the Lloyd's Law Reports series but also the Building Law Reports

- www.butterworths.co.uk/aller/index.htm – All England Direct: contains the All England Law Reports series
- www.alliott.butterworths.co.uk/construction – Construction Law Direct: contains a number of series related specifically to construction law.

12. Conclusion

Dr Robert Gaitskell, QC

As mentioned in Chapter 1, the purpose of this book is to give straightforward, practical advice to engineers on site as problems arise. Armed with the knowledge that is set out in this book, it will often be possible to avoid a dispute developing at all. For example, if the contract is drafted in a sensible and fair way, allocating risk to the party most able to bear and control it, the likelihood of disputes developing is immediately reduced. Similarly, if good records are kept on site then when factual disputes arise about, say, on what days bad weather delayed work, they can be quickly resolved by reference to the records. Similarly, properly maintained site minutes can serve a similar purpose.

However, if a dispute does arise, then it is essential that proper steps are taken at the proper time. Various chapters deal with the notices that need to be given, and model documents are provided to serve as useful checklists of the key ingredients necessary.

No matter that the engineer is located on an isolated site in a developing country, there is advice in Chapter 11 on how to access immediate help on the internet, as well as through books and libraries. All the advice in this book comes from practitioners who deal with such disputes on a daily basis and is underpinned by site experience.

In essence, this book aims to help any construction professional to avoid a dispute arising but, if one does materialise, it gives the tools for dealing with that dispute in the most cost effective and timely way. This book deals in detail with the seven available forms of dispute resolution and, in each case, identifies the circumstances where it is most appropriate and the features which distinguish it from the other processes available.

The contributors to this book trust that you, as a construction professional, will find it helpful. Whatever your experience of it, we would like to hear about it. All feedback will be gratefully received. We may be contacted at clerks@keatingchambers.com.

Index

Note: text in boxes is indicated by **emboldened page numbers**

active case management, 44
ad hoc arbitration, 59–60
adjudication, 2, 5, 73–91
  compared with other dispute resolution
    processes, 92, 110
  costs/offers, 85–86
  decision, 90
  enforcement of decision, 42, 90–91
  extension of time, 86, 87–88
  further submissions, 90
  jurisdictional points, 87, 91
  meetings, 86, 89–90
  notice, 80–82
  procedures, 89–90
  provisions under HGCR Act, 5, 17, 42,
    74–76
  referral notice, 83–86
  request for meeting or hearing, 86
  substantive part of response, 88–89
  technical use of, 77–79
  in various countries, 131–134
  written questions, 89
adjudication clauses (in contract), 18
adjudication enforcement proceedings, 42,
  90–91
  applications for declaratory relief, 42
adjudication proceedings, responding to,
  86–89
adjudication rules, 79–80
adjudicator
  appointment of, 82–83
    after dispute has arisen, 83
    prior to dispute, 82–83
  costs, 85–86
adjudicator nominating bodies, 83, **84**
admissible evidence, 52
alternative dispute resolution (ADR), 12,
  44–45
  costs resulting from refusal to take part,
    54–55

draft order, **45**
  see also early neutral evaluation;
    mediation
'ambush' adjudications, 77, 78–79, 86
appeals
  adjudication, 76, 90
  arbitration, 71
  litigation, 55
arbitration, 3–4, 56–72
  ad hoc, 59–60
  advantages over litigation, 3–4, 57–58
  ancillary/interim relief applications, 66
  appointing legal and technical advisors,
    123–124
  closing submissions, 68
  commencing, 60–61, 122–123
  compared with other dispute resolution
    processes, 3–4, 56–57, 92, 110, 111,
    112
  conducting, 64–66, 123–126
  costs, 69–70
    ways of limiting, 70
  disadvantages, 58
  disclosure obligations, 65
  documents, 64–65
  evidence gathering, 65, 125
  expert witnesses, 65
  factual witnesses, 65
  hearing, 66–68, 126
  institutional rules, 59, 121
  international disputes, 57, 60, 121–131
  letter before action, **62**
  meaning of term, 56
  mediation prior to, 95–96
  multi-party claims, 58, 61
  notice of, 61, **63**, 64
  opening submissions, 68
  pleadings, 124
  preparation for hearing, 67–68,
    125–126

arbitration (*continued*)
    procedural irregularity, appeal on basis
      of, 71–72
    right of appeal, 60
    timetable, 66, 68
    in various countries, 127–131
    video-link evidence, 126, **127**
    witness statements, 65, 125
    written submissions, 64
arbitration award, 68–69, 126–127
    appeal against, 71
    challenging, 70–72, 127
    enforcing, 69, 127
    final award, 68–69
    interest payable on, 69
    slip rule used to challenge, 70–71
arbitration claims, 38–42
    directions applicable, 41
    form used, 33, 39, **40–41**
    TCC practice, 41–42
arbitration clause (in contract), 18, 59, 60,
    120
arbitration tribunal
    choosing, 61–64
    compared with sole arbitrator, 62, 64
arbitrators
    appointment of, 60, 122–123
    number, 60, 61–62
    sole arbitrator compared with tribunal,
      62, 64
Australia
    adjudication in, 132
    arbitration in, 130–131

barristers, 21
    direct access schemes, 21–22, 24–28
      advantages, 24
      arrangements, 27–28
      cases suited to, 24, 25
      licensed access scheme, 24, 26
      public access scheme, 24, 26–27
      restrictions, 24, 27
      types, 24, 26–27
    fees, 22, 27
    restrictions on services offered, 24, 25
    services, 24–25
    unavailability due to other commitments,
      28
breach of contract, limitation period for, 61
Brussels Convention (1968), 112

case law, on standard forms of contract, 11
case management conference (CMC)
    documents, 43–44

information sheet, **43**
list of proposed directions, **44**
timing, 42, 43
cases cited
    abbreviations used for references,
      145–146
    Aiton Australia Pty Ltd v. *Transfield Pty
      Ltd* [1999], **13**
    Amec Civil Engineering v. *Secretary of
      State for Transport* [2004], 16, 17
    American Cyanamid v. *Ethicon* [1975],
      48
    *Bernard Schulte GMBH & Co. KG and
      others* v. *Nile Holdings Ltd* [2004],
      110
    Bouygues v. *Dahl-Jensen* [2000], 132
    British Steel Corporation v. *Cleveland
      Bridge Engineering Co. Ltd* [1984], **8,
      9**
    Butler Machine Tool Co. Ltd v. *Ex-Cell-O
      Corporation* [1979], **8–9**
    Cable & Wireless plc v. *IBM United
      Kingdom plc* [2003], 17
    Collins Contractors Ltd v. *Baltic Quay
      Management (1994) Ltd* [2005], 17
    Edward Campbell & Others v. *OCE (UK)
      Ltd* [2005], 114
    English v. *Emery Reimbold & Strick Ltd*
      [2002], 54
    Gillies Ramsay Diamond v. *PJW
      Enterprises Ltd* [2002], 79
    Halsey v. *Milton Keynes General NHS
      Trust* [2004], 45, 54
    Johnsey Estates Ltd v. *Secretary of State
      for the Environment, Transport and
      the Regions* [2001], 54
    Lesotho Highlands Development Authority
      v. *Impreglio SpA and Others* (2005),
      127
    McGlinn v. *Waltham Contractors Ltd*
      [2005], 33
    Macob Civil Engineering Ltd v. *Morrison
      Construction Ltd* [1999], 74
    McPhilemy v. *Times Newspapers Ltd (No.
      2) * [2004], 54
    Macro & Others v. *Thompson & Others,*
      111
    Mareva Compania Naviera SA v.
      International Bulkcarriers SA [1975],
      48
    Northern Developments v. *J & J Nichol*
      [2002], 85
    Northern RHA v. *Derek Crouch* [1984],
      110

Nottingham Building Society v. *Eurodynamics Systems* [1993], 48
Outwing v. *Randall* [1999], 76
Phonographic Performance Ltd v. *AEI Rediffusion Music Ltd* [1999], 54
R.G. Carter Ltd v. *Edmund Nuttall Ltd* (2000), 18
Rhodia Chirex Ltd v. *Laker Vent Engineering Ltd* [2004], 108
Scott Kem Ltd v. *Bentley* [1991], 47
Sir Lindsay Parkinson v. *Triplan Ltd* [1973], **53**
Smith v. *Peters* (1875), 112
Sudbrook Trading Estates Ltd v. *Eggleston and Others* [1983], 112
Swain v. *Hillman* [2001], 47
Tanfern Ltd v. *Cameron-MacDonald* [2000], 55
Thames Valley Power Ltd v. *Total Power & Gas Ltd* [2005], 110, 113, 114
Three Rivers District Council v. *Bank of England (No. 3)* [2001], 47
Transgri v. *Siemens* [2004], 132
Turriff Construction v. *Regalia Knitting Mills* [1971], **9**
Wates Construction v. *Franthom Property Ltd* [1991], **11–12**
William Verry (Glazing Systems) Ltd v. *Furlong Homes Ltd* [2005], 88
Zockoll Group Ltd v. *Mercury Communications Ltd* [1998], 48
cash flow, legislation to improve, 5, 74, 77
Centre for Dispute Resolution (CEDR)
address, **84**, **136**
as adjudicator nominating body, **84**
mediation services, 96, 136
Rules for Adjudication, 80
Chartered Institute of Arbitrators, as adjudicator nominating body, **84**
China, arbitration in, 127–129
China International Economic and Arbitration Commission (CIETAC), 127–129
civil courts, 143
Civil Procedure Rules (CPR), 3, 29, 143
objectives, 29, 42
claim
defending, 19–21
initiating, 17–19
making, 19
non-admission of, 16
claim forms, litigation, 33, **34**, 38
clarity, in expert determination, 113
company sale, dispute over, 114

complexity of dispute, choice of resolution procedures affected by, 19
conciliation, 4, 136
confidentiality, 18, 57, 92–93
Construction Industry Council (CIC), Model Adjudication Procedure, 79
consultants, advantages of Construction Act (1996), 79
contemporaneous records/documents, 14–15, 85
contract management, dispute avoidance by effective, 14–15
contract terms, clarity and fairness of, 10–11
contractors, advantages of Construction Act (1996), 77, 78, 79
contractual means of avoiding disputes, 7–14
costs
adjudication, 85–86
arbitration, 57, 69–70
legal/litigation, 22–23, 52–55
costs/proportionality
in arbitration, 70
choice of dispute resolution procedures affected by, 19
counterclaims, 36–37, 124
Court of Appeal, 55, 144
court litigation
meaning of term, 3
see also litigation
court system, 143–144
criminal courts, 143
Cyanamid guidelines, 48

deadline(s), 19–20
for responding to claim, 17, 20
deadlock (during negotiations), 102
ways of breaking, 102
direct access schemes *see* barristers, direct access schemes
disclosure obligations, 48–49, 65
dispute, meaning of term, 16–17
dispute avoidance, 7–15
contractual means, 7–14
by effective contract management, 14–15
dispute boards (DBs), 5, 120, 134–135
operating, 135
dispute resolution
choice of procedures, 2–6, 17–19
factors affecting, 18–19
control of procedures, 137
finally determinative procedures, 2, 3–4
preliminary procedures, 2, 4–5
traditional approach, 12

dispute resolution clause(s)
  misuse of, 137–138
  need to be well structured, 12–14
documents exchange, 48–49, 65, 124

early neutral evaluation (ENE), 4–5,
    115–119
  agreement covering, 117–118
  compared with other dispute resolution
      processes, 110, 115, 135–136
  evaluation decision/recommendation, 119
  features, 116
  meaning of term, 115
  preparation for evaluation, 118–119
  procedure, 118
  purpose, 116
  reasons for not suggesting in contract, 13
  when to use, 117
  see also evaluator
enforceability
  adjudication awards, 42
  arbitration awards, 57
engineer, meaning of term, 1
engineering institutions
  arbitration rules, 59–60
  standard forms of contract, **10**
engineers, advantages of Construction Act
    (1996), 79
evaluative procedures, 4, 95, 136
  see also conciliation
evaluator (in ENE)
  appointing, 117–118
  role of, 116
exclusion clauses, 21
expert determination, 4, 108–114
  advantages, 4
  benefits and risks, 109
  characteristics, 108, 111
  compared with other dispute resolution
      processes, 56–57, 110–113, 115
  for international disputes, 112–113, 137
  parties' agreement to refer dispute to,
      113–114
  procedure, 111–112
  questions to be answered by, 113
  reasons for not suggesting in contract,
      13
  valuation using, 109
expert reports, 50, **51**
expert witnesses, 65, 112
extension of time, 20

facilitative procedures, 4, 94, 135–136
  see also mediation

fees, legal, 22–23
FIDIC standard forms, dispute board
    provisions, 5, 134–135
finalised contract
  importance, 7–9
  results of not issuing, 8–9
finally determinative (dispute resolution)
    procedures, 2, 3–4, 55, 58
  see also arbitration; expert determination;
      litigation
flexibility/formality, arbitration hearings, 57
form of contract, disputes over, 8
freezing injunction, 48

hearsay evidence, 50
Hong Kong, adjudication in, 134
Hong Kong Airport Project, tiered dispute
    resolution process, 12–13
Hong Kong International Arbitration
    Centre, 134
House of Lords, 127, **128**, 144
Housing Grants, Construction and
    Regeneration Act (1996)
  adjudication provisions, 5, 17, 42, 75
  advantages for contractors, 77, 78, 79
  exclusions, 75
  notices, 77–78
  payment provisions, 5, 74, 77, 78
  Scheme for Construction Contracts, 75
    circumstances under which it applies,
        75, 77
    ways to avoid imposition of, 75–76
  Section 110 notice, 78
  statutory adjudication in, 5, 73, 74–76
  suspension of work by contractor allowed
      under, 78–79
  time provisions, 87–88
  withholding notice, 78

injunction, 47–48
Institution of Chemical Engineers (IChemE)
    standard forms of contract, **10**
    Adjudication Rules, 80
Institution of Civil Engineers (ICE)
    Adjudication Procedure, 80
    standard forms of contract, **10**
      dispute resolution clauses, 17
Institution of Mechanical Engineers and
    Institution of Electrical Engineers,
    standard forms of contract, **10**
institutional rules of arbitration, 59, 61,
    121
insurance, and standard forms of contract,
    11

International Bar Association (IBA)
  conflict-of-interest guidelines, **123**
  rules of evidence, **125**
International Chamber of Commerce
    (ICC)
  arbitration procedural rules, 59, 121, 124
    initiating arbitration under, 122,
      139–142
  dispute board rules and documents, 5,
    135
  expert determination services, 137
  International Centre for Expertise, 137
  International Court of Arbitration, 59,
    121, **122**
  mediation services, 136
international projects
  arbitration procedures used, 121–131
  choosing dispute resolution procedure,
    120–121
  dispute resolution in, 3, 57, 112–113,
    120–142

joinder of parties, in arbitration, 58
Joint Contracts Tribunal (JCT) standard
    forms of contract, **10**
  adjudication provisions, 73, 80
  example of clause amendments,
    11–12
  tiered dispute resolution clauses, 12
jurisdiction
  in adjudication, 87, 91
  in arbitration, 72
  challenge to, 36
  in litigation, 21
jurisdiction clause (in contract), 18

Keating Chambers, 2
  e-mail address, 149
  website, 2
Kendal, John, *Expert Determination* (book),
    111
Korea, South, arbitration in, 130

law reporting, 145
lawyers
  choosing, 22, 146
  communication lines agreed, 23–24
  fees, 22–23
    capped fees, 23
    contingency/success fees, 23
    fixed fees, 22, 27
    hourly rates, 22, 27
  instructing, 21–24
  see also barristers; solicitors

legal costs, 22–23
legal resources, 146–148
letter of claim, 19, **20**
  under TCC Pre-Action Protocol, 30,
    31–32
letter of intent, 7, 9
  enforceability, 9
limitation
  and arbitration, 61
  choice of dispute resolution procedures
    affected by, 18
litigation, 3, 29–55
  adjudication enforcement proceedings,
    42, 90–91
  appeals, 55
  arbitration claims, 33, 38–42
  case management, 42–44
  cases suited to, 29
  claim forms, 33, **34**
    for arbitration claims, 33, 39, **40–41**
    for Part 7 claims, 33, 42
    for Part 8 claims, 33, 38, 42
  commencement of proceedings, 33–42
  compared with other dispute resolution
    processes, 3–4, 56–57, 92, 110, 111,
    112
  costs, 52–55
    factors affecting, **53**
  counterclaim, 36–37
    defence to, 37
  defence to claim, 36
  disclosure, 48–49
  expert evidence, 50
  further pleadings, 37–38
  interim injunction, 47–48
  interim payment order, 47
  mediation prior to, 95–96
  order for costs, 54
  order for security, 53
  Part 7 claims, 33, 42
  Part 8 claims, 33, 38, 42
  Part 18 claims, 37
  Part 20 claims, 37
  Part 24 application, 46–47
  Part 36 offer, 53–54
  pre-action protocols, 19, 30–33
  pre-trial review, 51–52
  statement of truth, 36, 39
  statements of case, 33–37
  summary judgment, 45–47
  Technology and Construction Court
    (TCC) system, 3, 29–30
  trial procedures, 52
  witness statements, 49–50

London Court of International Arbitration
(LCIA), 59, 121, **122**
Lugano Convention (1988), 112

Malaysia
  adjudication in, 134
  arbitration in, 130
materials, standards on, 10
mediation, 2, 4, 92–107
  advantages, 4, 92–93
  characteristics, 92–93
  compared with other dispute resolution
    processes, 92, 110, 115, 135–136
  evaluative approach, 95
  facilitative approach, 4, 94
  facilities needed, 99
  initiating, 97–98, 136–137
  position papers/statements, 98
    sample, **104–107**
  preparation for, 98
  procedure, 97–103
    bargaining phase, 101–102
    concluding phase, 102–103
    exploration phase, 100–101
  reasons for not suggesting, 13, 116
  reasons for success, 93–94, 100
  success rate, 2, 4
  timing, 96
  when to use, 95–96
mediation clauses (in contract), 17–18
mediator
  appointment of, 96
    form of agreement for, **97**
  neutrality and impartiality, 93, 95
  role of, 93–94, 100
meteorological records, 14
multi-party arbitrations, 58, 61
multi-party mediations, 93

NEC Engineering & Construction Contract,
  10
  adjudication provisions, 80
neutrality, arbitration, 58
New York Convention (1958), 57, 127
  signatories, 112, 127, 128, 129, 130
New Zealand
  adjudication in, 132–133
  arbitration in, 131
notice of adjudication, 80–82
notice of arbitration, 61, **63**, 64

parallel proceedings, and arbitration,
  58
'pay when paid' clauses, 5, 74

payment by instalments, 77
per incuriam decision, 144
pre-action protocols, 19, 30–33
  information to be included, 32–33
  letter of claim, 30, **31–32**
  recovery of costs of complying with,
    33
  requirements, 30–31
pre-emptive remedies, in arbitration, 58
pre-trial review (PTR), 51–52
precedent, doctrine of, 144–145
preliminary (dispute resolution) procedures,
  2, 4–5
  see also adjudication; dispute boards;
    early neutral evaluation; mediation
privacy of hearings, 57, 92–93

quality of work
  defining of, 10
  disputes on, 9
quantum meruit basis of payment, 8
Queen's Bench Guide, on drafting of
  pleadings, 33–36

reality testing, 100, 116
records, importance of keeping, 14
reference sources, 146
references in case citations, 145–146

scope of work
  defining of, 10
  disputes on, 9
sealed offer, in arbitration, 70
Singapore
  adjudication in, 133–134
  arbitration in, 129
solicitors, 21
  choosing, 146
  fees, 22
  need for, 25–26
South Korea, arbitration in, 130
specific disclosure, 49
speed of resolution
  arbitration, 57–58
  choice of dispute resolution procedures
    affected by, 18, 57
standard forms of contract
  adjudication provisions, 80
  benefits, 11
  disputes reduced by using, 10–11
  examples listed, **10**
statutory adjudication, 5, 73, 74–76
  in various countries, 132–133
staying of court proceedings, 21

summary judgment, 45–47, 136
  reasons for, 45–46
Swiss Chambers of Commerce, 121, **122**

Taiwan, arbitration in, 131
technical expertise, in arbitration, 57
Technology and Construction Bar
    Association, as adjudicator nominating
    body, **84**
Technology and Construction Court (TCC),
    3, 29–30, 143
  adjudication enforcement proceedings,
    42
  arbitration claims procedure, 41–42
  classification of cases, 30
  disclosure rules, 49
  early neutral evaluation encouraged by,
    119
  expert reports, 50
  Part 24 application, 46–47
Technology and Construction Solicitors
    Association (TeCSA)
  Adjudication Rules, 80
  as adjudicator nominating body, **84**
tiered dispute resolution process, 12–13
  reason for adopting, 13, 137
time extension, 20

United Nations Commission on
    International Trade Law
    (UNCITRAL)
  arbitration procedural rules, 59, 121, 131
  Model Law, 121
    national legislation based on, 127, 130,
    131

video conferencing facilities, **127**
video-link evidence, 126

Washington Convention, signatories to, 129,
    130
websites
  arbitration appointing bodies, **122**
  information sources, 147–148
  mediation services, **136**
  professional organisations, 26, **123**
withholding notice, 78
witness conferencing, 126
witness statements, 49–50
working relationships
  choice of dispute resolution procedures
    affected by, 18
  with lawyers, 23–24
World Bank funded projects, adjudication
    provisions, 5, 134